Costly Mission

Following Christ into the slums

LINCOLN CHRISTIAN COLLEGE AND SEMINARY

Michael Duncan

MARC

121 East Huntington Drive, Monrovia, California 91016-3400 USA

Costly Mission: Following Christ into the Slums

Michael Duncan

ISBN 0-912552-96-4

Published by MARC, a division of World Vision International, 121
East Huntington Drive, Monrovia, California 91016-3400, U.S.A.
First published by World Vision Australia in 1995 as *Development,
Discipleship and Pain.*

Printed in the United States of America. Editor and page layout:
Edna Valdez. Cover design: Richard Sears. Photos: Michael Duncan.

CONTENTS

Gratius, St. o

Foreword

In July 1993, twenty-five people took part in an "Aid and Development in Mission" course, one of the programs of the School of World Mission at Whitley College in Melbourne, Australia.

During the first week of the course, we were privileged to sit with Michael Duncan as he bared his soul and reflected on the joys and pain of serving the poor in the name of Christ. It was a five-day emotional roller coaster. Together we laughed, cried, became angry, were humbled, amazed, rejoiced in God's goodness and gnashed our teeth at Satan's destructiveness.

Michael was unusually transparent, taking us into the nooks and crannies of his heart. He ruthlessly exposed the failures he saw in his own self, and described the unexpected bumps and sidetracks in the journey that left him clinging by his fingertips to the challenge, "hope in God." We were moved at such honesty, and humbled by the truth that Christians in service still have many lessons to learn and many more mistakes to make.

Michael has rewritten those presentations into this book. To make the story coherent he has sometimes used portions of the material from his *Journey in Development,* to which this is a sequel [*Journey in Development* is part of the series of publications called "The Bridge," published by World Vision Australia. –Ed.].

His was no human success story, but it gave us the assurance that God is at work in Michael and in those of us who shared with him. I believe the Lord will continue that work as you read, reflect and relate these insights to your situation.

Finally, this book is dedicated to Bonnie Cormack, who participated in the course where this material was first presented. Bonnie passed into God's presence in October 1995.

John Steward
World Vision Australia

Preface

The journey in this book spans decades. It is my hope that I have remembered and recorded events as accurately as possible. I cannot guarantee this and humbly apologize for any exaggerations, distortions or inaccuracies that may exist.

To protect certain individuals, I have changed their names and employed license to disguise their identity and circumstances. Mary, the main character in this book, must be identified as a representative person. Many of the incidents I have related did happen to a person I know, but I have intentionally left out some things and added others to conceal her identity. While all the events described are factual, they did not necessarily happen to one person.

Finally, I must state that the journey which Ruby and I have taken is not necessarily representative of the journeys undertaken by our former colleagues in Servants to Asia's Urban Poor.

The Journey Begins

In 1972 the last of New Zealand's forces pulled out of Vietnam. This added to my growing disillusionment with "the system." I began to ask why there was so much poverty in the world. To say the least, this is a most disturbing and threatening question. I asked the question as a non-Christian; tragically it is not being asked by many Christians today.

Many Christians seem to have lost the ability to ask the hard questions—those that profoundly disturb and shake their comfortable Christian understandings. It has been said that we grow when we are threatened. I hope that as you read this book, threatening questions arise that, in the answering, help you to grow.

Radical roots

I was unable to ignore this and other questions, so after explaining this to my family, I set out on a pursuit of truth. This took me into the world of the humanities at university, then drugs and the hippie culture; from there I travelled as a recluse—a loner withdrawn from society—and indulged in Eastern mysticism.

In 1975, I arrived in Christchurch on New Zealand's South Island. I had nowhere to live. A big, burly Christian named Bruce White—a dedicated Jesus person—took me into his house. For the next seven months he fed me a diet of Bible, Bible and books about the Bible. While in the hippie culture, I blamed the world's woes on "the system." But reading the Bible introduced me to another cause: me! Jesus talked of changing my selfishness and the system. In becoming a Christian I could experience personal transformation and still be a rebel. I had to leave a destructive counterculture and join Jesus' counterculture.

On Easter Monday morning in 1976, I knelt in my cold little room and spoke the following dangerous sentences: "Lord Jesus, forgive me. Change me and use me to change the world." Walking down the corridor a minute later, I felt that I was indeed a new person with a new life. Turning toward Jesus meant turning away from drugs, the occult and Eastern mysticism. In telling my story to young people I am often greeted with attentive ears but told that my story is dated—that being a hippie is no longer culturally relevant. But it seems to me that the evils of drugs, occultism and mysticism are no more ugly than the cultures of "me-ism," hedonism and consumerism. Turning to Jesus and accepting his priorities is a way to live above and beyond all these insidious "isms."

I was no different from thousands of other seekers. We felt that the age of enlightenment—with its belief in science, reason and progress—had failed us. A new age was needed.

Through Jesus we heard and saw the possibility of the future kingdom of God invading the present. This gave us hope, purpose and meaning. Jesus made it very clear that as his followers we were not to seek personal satisfaction, but to serve. Coming to Jesus did mean receiving new life but it also meant giving our lives to others for the rest of our lives. We came to the Lord Jesus as rebels and Jesus did not turn us into conservative nice people. Rather, he turned us toward his creation, the world, to recreate it.

I can repeat my story a thousand times over. Others working for Christ include former drug dealers and addicts, occultists, gang members, hippies, rockers and moral failures of all descriptions. We have all been washed clean by Jesus!

But Jesus washed us clean that we may serve. We all soon learned that our respective healings were not for us, but for others. We had been set free to serve others. This is a far cry from what people hear today. Pastors, evangelists and healers call for the hurting to come forward to be healed and set free. So far so good. Your healing, these preachers urge, will make you whole and happy. This is a half-truth. Healing is wholeness, but at the end of the day, God is not too interested in our happiness; that is not his primary concern. Rather, God heals so we can serve him and live for others. Our healing is not for us, but for God, his purposes and those less fortunate than us.

As God revealed these truths to us, we became people out of step with many of our contemporaries. While they were seeking to actualize themselves, we were seeking to deny ourselves. Some charged us with fanaticism; we accepted that charge gladly. We unashamedly wanted to rebel against the way of the world that so easily impoverishes people. All we wanted to do was to change the world to the way of Jesus. We were optimistic. We believed we could make a difference!

Walking with Jesus

The day after praying that dangerous prayer to Jesus I got thoroughly depressed. It was as though big black clouds of woe came tumbling down on me. This was a far cry from the love, joy and peace that others said I could expect. This was a very confusing time. It was as though a thousand voices were speaking to me, many of them urging me to give up Jesus. I mentioned this to a pastor, Murray Robertson, who suggested it may be related to my past and prayed for me for the next two hours. It was as though many chains fell off me, one at a time. It was a very liberating and healing experience that continues even to this day.

I am extremely grateful that Jesus used Murray to bring about this personal transformation. Working among the very poor is a heavy enough load without carrying around many deep emotional hurts or festering wounds from substance abuse. These disabilities can severely limit our journey with the poor, as we must travel lightly. We must be sufficiently free so that we may serve.

I began attending Murray's church, and on one particular Sunday was challenged to give some of my hard-earned wages to their missionary venture. At the time I was working at a paper bag factory making the glue that sealed the bottom of the bag. Each church member was asked to pray about the size of their offering. After some prayer, I settled on a large percentage of my wages as my offering to the missionary endeavor. I was single and had few responsibilities. There were times, however, when I was short of money and on one occasion I could not afford a much needed pair of socks. I faithfully and prayerfully took this problem to the Almighty. Some days later I was given a suit by a friend at a secondhand clothing store. I couldn't believe it. Surely God wouldn't mix the orders up. I had asked for a pair of socks, not a suit! But I took the suit home and searched the pockets for forgotten money. Believe it or not, in one pocket I found a brand new pair of socks!

This story has a purpose. You may, after reading it, charge me with being too simplistic and call me a naive and reckless young believer. Maybe so. But I wonder if many "older" Christians have become pale copies of their "new" Christian selves, no longer excited by their faith or their God. Have they lost that ability to have a reckless love affair with God, to be fools, but for his glory?

Glad to go

During the next few years after my prayer encounter with the pastor and release from the chains of my past, I married Ruby Davies and went to Bible college. Ruby and I spent a few years serving others as pastors in a local Baptist church.

We began to sense a calling to serve the marginalized squatters of Asia and were encouraged in this by some friends. We would take our two-year-old, Emily, and nine-month-old Thomas to Manila and live in a slum.

It was crazy, really. Some charged us with ignorance and others with arrogance. We were told by other mission leaders that our intentions would come to nothing. But we knew that history was on our side. Throughout the centuries, humanity has been changed by daring minorities. In God's scheme of things, several unassuming and insignificant people could make a difference. That was our hope.

As we studied the Bible, we read of God's heart for the poor and his cry for justice. By choosing to serve the poor we knew we were following Scripture. It was not as though God was commanding us to go to the shanties of Asia. We were not obeying some law by choosing a life among the poor, nor were we embarking on a great campaign based on massive research to identify needs and match resources. We were glad to be Christians! We had experienced the grace of God, his forgiveness, healing and love. Giving our lives to the poor of Asia was simply our response to that grace.

It was one thing to be grateful at heart, but quite another to board an airplane and then move to a slum. But that is what we decided to do—to actually place ourselves in a poor community in imitation of what Jesus had done.

Jesus the scandal

Jesus was becoming a dangerous example for us to follow. As we read, reread and read the Gospels again, we
encountered a different Jesus. This was a Jesus not just
located safely in print on the pages of the Bible nor a
Jesus on a golden cross between two candles on an ornate
altar in a safe church building. Instead, we saw a Jesus
walking, acting and living, a Jesus living an earthly life
between the time of his virgin birth and his ugly crucifix-
ion. It was a life spent touching others: walking, talking,
laughing, crying, working, drinking, eating, travelling, listening, praying, healing and debating. More significantly
we saw Jesus mixing with those considered "bad company" by the elite of his day—with the underclass, the
social casualties, the widows, orphans, unemployed, sick
and deviants. He was often with those deemed rude,
untutored and unlettered, hated and scorned by others.

Jesus the scandal—always with the wrong people at the
wrong time in the wrong places! The scandal of our times
is that many Christians begin movements from above
with the "right" people in the "right" places.

Far from excluding the rich, Jesus' love and justice
promised to liberate the rich and powerful from the
actions that so often disempower the poor. For example,
the apostle Luke tells us of the difference Jesus made in
the life of the rich man, Zacchaeus. Ultimately, however,
Jesus sides with those who have no one else to defend
them. His priority is those people with the least.

In Manila we hoped to do likewise—at times to mix
with the rich, especially rich Christians, to create some
understanding about the poor. But we would do this from
a position of poverty. In other words, we would not
become like the rich so as to communicate to them but
live in a way that would prophetically challenge them. It

should be no surprise that the one person who seems to challenge the rich today more than anyone else is herself a poor person who lives with the dying. Her name is Mother Teresa.

We applied to Servants to Asia's Urban Poor.[1] We would go to Asia not with an imperialistic motive, to conquer the "natives" for Jesus. Nor would we go with a cultural motive, to impose Western culture on another people; nor with a romantic motive, to get away and escape from New Zealand so as to be with an "exotic" people; nor with a motive of ecclesiastical colonialism to export one's own confession and church to another territory.[2] Instead, we would go to be with the poor and to serve them.

We had God on our side, each other, hearts full of gratefulness and compassion, the beginnings of a model, a place to start and a family of friends in Servants. Now all that was required was to actually do it. To begin to walk the walk. Obedience to a radical mandate came down to an act of the will and a bodily response.

NOTES

1 Servants to Asia's Urban Poor is an outgrowth of the charismatic movement in New Zealand and works incarnationally in a number of Asian cities. I refer to it as "Servants" or "the Servants organization" in the rest of this book.

2 These motivational categories are found in David Bosch, *Transforming Mission: Paradigm Shifts in Theology of Mission* (Maryknoll: Orbis, 1992), p. 5.

A Slum Is Born

We joined Servants to Asia's Urban Poor and set out for the slums of Manila, arriving in the midst of a typhoon. Perhaps this was an indication of what was in store for us over the next couple of years.

On our arrival we were greeted by the sight of two burly, macho, gun-carrying policeman coming toward us. They simply asked if everything was all right. During our first night in the Servant's Retreat Center we were awakened by Colin Harrington calling us downstairs to help evacuate valuable equipment from five feet of filthy floodwater.

The day came when we had to pack our few belongings and move to the slum. Upon arriving at the slum, Colin helped us to unload and then departed. Ruby and I, with our two little ones, were left standing in our new home. We did not know the language, did not know a soul, and in this stark setting did not know how to cook, sleep or even bathe the children. As Colin faded into the distance I stood there and cried. I felt utterly out of control. This feeling remained with me for the next year. I was scared! Ruby, on the other hand, was so stunned by it all that she simply attended to her duties. Day-to-day survival became our agenda for much of that first year. There just wasn't enough emotional energy to give ourselves adequately to learning the language and understanding the culture and social issues of the community where we now lived.

Every time I heard an airplane fly over I wished I was on it. Our missionary furlough in New Zealand in three years' time seemed a lifetime away. It was as though we were "doing time" in jail. And, as often happens in jail, we were suddenly relocated. Because of personnel changes in the Servants organization our team decided, with our agreement, that we should go to another slum community called Damayan Lagi, which means "always helping."

Damayan Lagi

Within a week we found a house in Damayan Lagi. It was not the home of our dreams but we found it livable. Our two plywood rooms shared walls with adjoining houses. The wooden floor had a gaping hole revealing a rat-infested sewerage pit which could be covered when not in use.

After the first day the novelty of being in a new place was over. In many respects Damayan Lagi was just like the slum we had left. Yet again we were surrounded by thousands of people, filthy conditions, vermin and insecurity.

Often, visitors to Damayan Lagi ask how such a place came into existence in the first place. These are the stages of Damayan Lagi's history (see also Figure 2.1 on page 11).

Act One: Mary

Mary, our landlady, was poor because she had always been poor. Her mother had bequeathed her life and poverty. At the marriage altar, Mary brought this poverty to her equally poverty-stricken husband, who could only pledge more of the same. Forced by this reality to marry within their class, these two lives were joined in poverty.

As husband and wife they squatted on the Mandelina Estate, the part of Manila that later became known as Quezon City. Their first house, a crude hut made of bamboo and nipa[1] and whatever else nature could furnish, was near a river that became their source of fish and water. Their closest neighbors were many meters away. Far from idyllic, this beginning was rugged and unkind. Poverty, even in a landscape of tranquility, is still poverty.

Mary can still recall how the owner of the land, a rich foreigner whose family had come to the Philippines chasing more wealth, used to ride around on his fine horse. Not content to be a landowner, he ran for Congress and lost. His political debts were such that he had to pawn his land to the banks. Eventually he returned to his homeland and the banks took over the ownership of the estate.

Mary, losing ground on so many fronts, knew very little of the political maneuverings that had affected the ownership of the land she lived on. She did, however, get word to family and friends in the provinces telling them of land that they could squat on. They came, with many other urban hopefuls around the world to be part of one of the greatest treks of the twentieth century: the rural-urban migration.

Coming by foot and in small groups, they were barely noticed as they arrived on the estate. These little people were of no significance to the bankers. They quietly dotted the land with their rough nipa huts. Even after World War II, when Manuel Quezon, then president of the Philippines, scanned this area for his dream city, these little people did not count for much. All President Quezon could see was enormous space to house the government, commerce and people in style and spacious surroundings.

Act Two: Marcos

Ironically, the poor became very visible when in 1965 Ferdinand Edralin Marcos came to power. Marcos had the ability to squeeze money from the rich and votes from the poor. Upon assuming power he immediately targeted the Communist resurgence in the countryside for destruction. His strategy was to use the land as his weapon by developing the rural sector through new strains of rice, fertilizers and mechanized farming, and thereby destroy the Marxists' power base. His "Green Revolution" initially achieved high yields, and by 1967 the country was producing enough rice to meet local needs. But unfortunately for Marcos and for Mary, this success came at a terrible cost.

The development program favored a capital-intensive production system over a labor-intensive system. This

Figure 2.1: The making of a slum

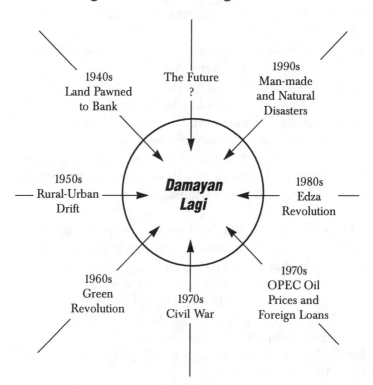

1940s
Land Pawned
to Bank

The Future
?

1990s
Man-made
and Natural
Disasters

1950s
Rural-Urban
Drift

*Damayan
Lagi*

1980s
Edza
Revolution

1960s
Green
Revolution

1970s
Civil War

1970s
OPEC Oil
Prices and
Foreign Loans

meant the Green Revolution favored the landowners with money, not the landless workers; the skilled who could make the shift to mechanized farming, not the unskilled. The latter were laid off in the thousands. In the words of one landlord: "If you tell a machine to do something, it will do it. It's not that way with tenants."[2] Those who were fortunate to find employment usually signed on as day laborers at low wages.[3] By the time martial law was imposed in 1971, possibly half of all rural Filipino workers were living below the poverty line.[4]

Tens of thousands of these people trekked to the cities, and some found their way to the spacious Mandelina estate, Mary's home. It is estimated that during the 1960s the number of squatters in Manila increased from 60,000 to over 800,000. From landlessness to landlessness they came. Overnight Mary became neighbor to many newcomers. Gradually the green open spaces evolved into a crude and ugly cardboard city. Squatter hovels blotted the landscape, the river became the community rubbish dump, the open fields were lost in a maze of shanties, and the once useful pathways were now muddy, disease-ridden sewerage outlets and the only places for children to play.

Quezon's dream city was fast becoming a nightmare squatter town. Marcos' Green Revolution had produced places of death and the puny, insignificant poor were now powerfully present.

Over the years, floods, humidity, vermin, meager meals and disease had become Mary's constant companions. Her husband lived in fear of losing his job, and she knew she had lost her looks, figure and teeth in the harshness of it all. She feared that this would be her lot for the rest of her life. Every day she felt the same, with no hope of reversal. And what of the children? Over the years they had spilled from her belly and filled the house. Was this to be their fate as well?

The maze of Damayan Lagi

At the same time the daily radio and newspaper reports reminded her of the luxury and indulgence else-where in Manila. With every report her expectations of life rose. She yearned to be a consumer. But the gap was too great. What the media promised she would never have. Travelling their predetermined course, tears of tiredness and resignation—yet again—began to fall down her cheeks.

The poor cried out for a savior, someone who could deliver them from their poverty. Marcos, demonized by power, had become a peddler of death. In his second term as president, Marcos knew that constitutionally he could not seek a third term. Beyond December 30, 1973, he would have no power. And it galled him that his most likely successor was the leading senator, the young Benigno Aquino. Marcos orchestrated a strategy to stay in power. On August 21, 1971, opposition party candidates, spectators and members of the press were brutally killed or maimed in a grenade attack at a pre-election rally at the Miranda Plaza.

Marcos blamed the savage attack on the Communists, who subsequently denied any involvement. At that time the New People's Army, the military wing of the Communist party, only numbered a few hundred riflemen, and they were running for their lives in the hills from thousands of well-equipped soldiers. Subsequent evidence strongly suggested that Marcos and his top military advisor, General Fabian Ver, had masterminded the massacre. It was all part of their design to create chaos and fear in the hearts of the people, to engineer an excuse to impose martial law and thus retain power.

Students, sensing that something was about to happen, took to the streets in mass demonstrations. Their president responded with tanks and bullies. Hundreds were brutalized. "Are the Marxists right?" the students wondered. Had Marcos turned fascist, and were they now witnessing the self-destruction of capitalism? They were sure of one thing. The hour demanded action. Justice was at stake.

Justice was the last thing Marcos seemed interested in as he scrambled for power. On September 21, 1971, he issued Proclamation 1081, placing the Philippines under martial law.

To keep his American allies happy, Marcos justified his actions in the name of the Communist threat. The Americans, in their "red fever," understood. Furthermore, Marcos labelled his actions "martial law with a smile." As proof, he pointed out that he had not stormed the streets with tanks and troops. The Americans smiled. However,

people began to disappear. Senator Aquino was the first
of thousands to be arrested. He vanished. To cut short a
heroic story, Aquino was released then forced into exile
in the United States.

This was all irrelevant to Mary. Her main concern was
finding enough food for the next meal. Rice, not political
proclamations, was her worry. Aquino, for all his misfor-
tune, was still from a rich, landed family. And as for the
students, they were simply throwing away the sort of
good education she wished her children could have. But
education would prove to be the least of her worries in
the months ahead. Life itself was being weighed in the
balance.

Act Three: The Arabs, Swiss and Americanos

It was 1979, and the sheiks of the Middle East were
about to shock the world by raising oil prices once again.
These oil producers had become enormously influential
since 1973, when OPEC had quadrupled the price of oil.
Ferdinand Marcos worried over balance of payment
problems. Importing oil was proving very expensive and
foreign reserves were low, due to the recession in the
industrialized countries that affected the demand for
goods from the Philippines.

It came as no surprise when Mary's husband stooped
through the door one day and slumped onto the dirt
floor. "There are no more export orders," he whispered.
Like a man with a death sentence he announced that he
had been laid off. An awful silence filled the room. Mary
did not know whether to look at her unemployed husband, the floor or the statue of Jesus in the corner. Once
again their lot in life had been determined by decisions
made elsewhere.

Marcos knew where to turn for help. The foreign
banks would give him loans. The banks, many of them

American, were full to overflowing with Middle Eastern petrodollars. They were falling over one another in their eagerness to lend to developing nations.[5] Some of the white collar minds in the financial centers had decided that, just as a massive injection of American capital had helped Germany after World War II, so the process could be repeated in the Third World. Germany had been so devastated that its condition resembled that of an under-developed country, and the Marshall Aid plan helped restore Germany to economic health. Why not do for the Philippines what had proven so successful in Germany?[6]

From each loan, Marcos allegedly pocketed his per-centages and commissions. These were quickly deposited in secretive Swiss banks, where no questions would be asked. This immoral lust for money by both Marcos and the Swiss banks was justified in the name of personal rights. The Swiss believed that everyone was entitled to their privacy.

Unfortunately, the Philippines had to repay the debts. Marcos faced some stark policy decisions. Cuts in domes-tic spending followed. These cuts crippled medical ser-vices to the poor—at the very time Mary desperately needed them. One of her children had bronchitis. Inces-sant coughing gave way to a high fever. The child was becoming listless and refused to eat. His once active body could no longer combat the infection within his lungs. Pneumonia set in.

It was urgent that Mary get her son to a hospital so he could receive intravenous fluids. Her poverty had already caused her humiliation at the doors of one hospital. Access to the medical world was denied her. Resigned to the inevitable, she watched her child slowly die.

The oil crisis robbed her husband of a job, then death took her little boy. Meanwhile, the rich were still on the fairways playing golf instead of creating jobs; the politicians stood on their platforms mouthing promises never to be kept; and priests, pastors and prophets in their pulpits preached abundant life after death, but not before.

Act Four: Benigno Aquino

One man, far from aspiring to be a savior, believed that the Filipino was worth dying for. Benigno (Ninoy) Aquino, still in America, was warned not to return to the Philippines, but knew that he must. His land was blighted, made rotten by Marcos and his corrupting use of brute power and military might.

On August 21, 1983, Flight 811 taxied to a stop at Gate 8 at the airport in Manila, with Benigno Aquino on board. Military units surrounded the plane. Six soldiers then proceeded to board the plane.

"Boss, the armed forces are inviting you," a soldier said in Tagalog to Aquino.

"Where are we going?" Ninoy asked.

"Just here," the soldier replied. "Please come with me."

As Ninoy left the plane and was escorted toward a side exit, eyewitnesses said his smile suddenly disappeared. "Sadness appeared across his face. He bit his lips. The most dreaded of fears must have crossed his mind."[7]

Seconds later, a shot rang out. Ninoy fell to the tarmac, dead. He had been shot in the back of the head. Before his departure for the Philippines, Ninoy had typed a brief statement. One paragraph stood out:

> According to Gandhi, the willing sacrifice of the innocent is the most powerful answer to insolent tyranny that has yet been conceived by God and man.[8]

Over two million people walked in the rain to Aquino's funeral. Ninoy's epitaph was also reported: "Is the Filipino worth dying for?" he had asked three years earlier. "I have come to the conclusion he is worth dying for, because he is the nation's greatest resource."

Marcos, blamed for Aquino's assassination, chose to face the people in the election of 1986. His opponent, a housewife, was dubbed by the press as "the saint," and Marcos, "the sinner." Mrs. Corazon (Cory) Aquino, the wife of Benigno, had managed to unite the opposition parties against Marcos and this group now threatened Marcos. As the votes came in it appeared that Mrs. Aquino had won. Contrary to all estimates, however, Marcos was declared the winner. The people charged him with massive fraud and poured onto the streets. Millions marched down Edza, the main highway in Manila, to oppose the rule of Marcos.

After a week of demonstrations, prayer and negotiation, it was all over. A chorus of singing and praying Filipinos brought Marcos tumbling down. After twenty years of tyrannical rule, Ferdinand and Imelda Marcos were forced to flee from the Philippines.

Mary had heard the news. Like many of the poor she could not help but be cynical about it all. The elite were simply having another of their political spats. The Aquino family was now replacing the Marcos family. The elite were still in power. Life would continue as it was. Powerful families, wealthy businessmen and the emerging middle class may have marched on Edza; but would they walk down the alleys of the slums and bring about an economic revolution?

She remembered the awful days and weeks surrounding Ninoy's assassination and knew that the months ahead would see a repetition of events. The assassination crisis had brought out the worst in the wealthy. They had reacted with panic buying, while all Mary could do was simply panic. The rich had emptied supermarkets, gasoline stations and their bank accounts, and closed their businesses. The capital flight from the Philippines had amounted to millions of dollars. Consequently, the peso dropped in value and prices soared. Mary could hardly purchase a thing.

And now, with Cory Aquino just installed in power, the same events were occurring. Mary was forced to buy less with her few pesos. From now on, it would be one or two meager meals a day, meals consisting of salty rice and a few pieces of fish. Mary read that the so-called Edza Revolution had been a bloodless one. "Let them come to our slums," she said to a friend, "and then they will see how bloody these revolutions can be!"

Act Five: Acts of God

Five years later, it seemed as if God had deserted the Philippines, especially as far as the poor were concerned. Cory Aquino, the saint, was receiving one disaster after another from the hand of her God. Typhoons, floods, earthquakes and volcanic eruptions tore into her country, scattering the poor everywhere. Some landed in Damayan Lagi with their horror stories.

Mary was stunned by what she was hearing. Belin, and many like her, had arrived from the flood-hit Ormoc City, on the central Philippines island of Leyte. "The smell of death was everywhere," Belin told Mary. "At the last estimate there were over five thousand dead!"

Mary had seen the Manila newspapers—papers with photos of bloated bodies lying everywhere, the despairing eyes of bereaved families, the demolished houses. Such was the death toll that there was no time for ceremony and people had run out of coffins, so bulldozers pushed the scattered bodies and rubbish into huge graves.

"One woman," continued Belin, "was walking home when the flood water became neck-deep. When she got home, she no longer had a house. Her husband had been preparing lunch for the children when the huge flood came. Her eight-year-old boy was able to scramble to safety on the roof but her husband and three of their children died, and three others were missing."[9]

Another story told of how Donlita Aldieno saw her thirteen-year-old daughter lose hold of a coconut tree and disappear. "She was crying for help but I couldn't do anything," said the distraught mother, who also lost her eighteen-month-old baby. Another, Estelito Balaro, grabbed hold of a log and did not let go as the flood waters carried off his family's thatch hut. His wife and daughter disappeared quickly. His two young sons clung to him until they could no longer hold on.

As always, people struggled to interpret these events within the framework of their faith. Some ardent Catholics blamed the disaster on the fact that many in Ormoc had recently converted to the "Born Again" religion, and God was punishing the city for an act of backsliding. The "Born Agains," on the other hand, blamed the disaster on President Cory Aquino and the Catholics, for their having dedicated the country to Mary, the Mother of God, after the 1986 Edza Revolution. This act of idolatry, they charged, resulted in God withdrawing his blessing from the country.

The rich businessmen and corrupt military personnel and government officials could only smile as this religious war was being fought, for it was they who had a big hand in the disaster. God, the Devil, the Catholics and the "Born Agains" were not to blame for the Ormoc disaster. Over the years, the greedy, corrupt, wealthy elite had indulged in illegal logging that reduced the hills surrounding Ormoc to barren lands without any trees to absorb the monsoon rains. During the heavy rains there was nothing to hold the hillsides together, so the mud and water fell on Ormoc below.

Mary had brought her family to Damayan Lagi. Marcos had brought the rural poor. The Arabs, Swiss and American banks brought further misery. The Aquinos brought political emancipation but not economic liberation. And the heavens and the earth brought disaster. People like Mary could only wonder what the future would bring.

A word to the reader

When working with a particular community of poor people, it is important to remember that we go to join their story, a story of many years. It is vital that we understand their story and where they have come from if we are to be effective in our development work with them. Karl Marx said that it is not enough to interpret the world but to change it. In order to change the world, however, we need first to rightly interpret the world. This involves not only sharing the pain on the streets with the people but also enduring the pain in the study as we dig into history books. We are to love the Lord and the people with our bodies in sacrificial service on the streets, but also with our minds in books.

To help me understand the context of Damayan Lagi, I not only sought to comprehend their history, but also their culture and religion. Furthermore, I also studied their households, their way of life and last, but not least, the poor themselves. All of this reflective activity proved invaluable for the following reasons.

First, how we perceive the poor will often determine how we treat them (see Figure 2.2 on page 22). For example, paternalism often has its roots in an inappropriate categorization of the poor. The poor will quickly discern what we really think of them. Discernment is necessary to survive in their cramped conditions, and the poor become remarkably accurate. This ability to discern

Figure 2.2: Understanding the poor

Understanding the poor means understanding the following categories of poverty.

1. **Popular Conceptions**
   - ❖ Happy Poor
   - ❖ Lazy Poor
   - ❖ Unfortunate Poor
   - ❖ Irresponsible Poor
   - ❖ Idealized Poor

2. **Theological Categories**
   - ❖ Old Testament words such as *chaser, yaresh, dal, ebyon* and *ani*
   - ❖ New Testament concepts of poverty: Luke 6:20 and Matthew 5:3

Luke 6	**Matthew 5**
Material Poverty	Spiritual Poverty
Poor Ones	Pious Ones
Suffering	Piety
Sociology	Religion
Left	Right
Deliverance from Misery	Deliverance from Sin

   Need a synthesis to see that Matthew 5 does not exclude economic considerations. Those who call out to God in their spirits are often those who suffer from material hardship.
   - ❖ Sinners and Sinned Against
   - ❖ Voluntary or Enforced Poverty

3. **Psychological Categories**
   - ❖ Subjects or Objects
   - ❖ Actors or Victims

4. **Sociological Categories**
   - ❖ Near Poor
   - ❖ Entrepreneurial Poor
   - ❖ Self-employed Poor
   - ❖ Laborers
   - ❖ Ultra-vulnerable poor (women and children)

5. **Economic Categories**
   - ❖ Subsistence Poverty
   - ❖ Relative Poverty
   - ❖ The Poor as People

Why study all of this? How we see the poor, how we perceive and define them will determine how we treat them, react to them and interact with them.

determines to what extent people are for or against the development worker. If we have not done our homework and have not rightly understood the poor and their context, they will pick that up and be very wary of us.

Second, understanding the history and context of the poor helps us to apportion blame where it truly belongs (see Figure 2.3 on page 24). Often in development work the temptation is to either blame ourselves for everything that is not happening or to blame the poor. But just a glance at the history of Damayan Lagi is enough to signal that there are international, national and local factors beyond our control that have caused much of the heartache and therefore share in the blame. An understanding of your context helps you to be morally responsible in attributing blame where it belongs.

Third, appreciating the wider picture also helps establish our context. A bedeviling attitude in much development work is to think that at the end of the day everything depends on the development worker. This becomes an unbearable burden. The wider picture helps us to see that if we are to address the problem of poverty effectively, we must also challenge some of the international, national and local players to do their part. It is as much their responsibility as ours.

Finally, I suspect that much of the one-eyed work where one "just does mercy," or "just seeks justice," or "just provides income generation" stems from a belief that we can locate the cause of poverty in one factor. But a family of factors contributes to the mess of poverty, and by seeing this our mission mandate must be holistic and engage all these factors. The wider picture gives birth to a broader mandate.

Unfortunately, when I moved into Damayan Lagi I had not done this necessary homework. I would pay dearly for this oversight.

Figure 2.3: Understanding your context

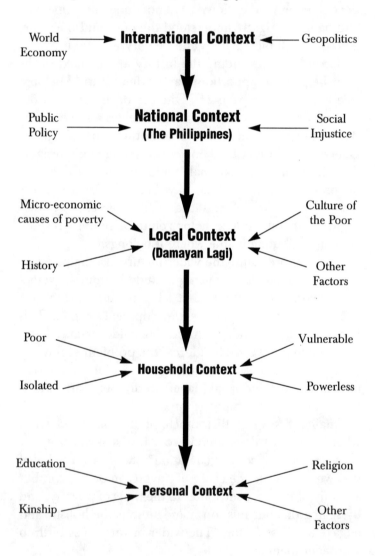

Understanding your context will mean
understanding the above dimensions.

NOTES

1 Nipa is a type of palm tree; its fronds are woven to create shelter.

2 Benedict J. Kerkvliet, ed., *Political Change in the Philippines: Studies of Local Politics Preceding Martial Law* (Honolulu: University of Hawaii Press, 1974), p. 20.

3 It is estimated that the number of farm laborer families rose from 444,000 in 1961 to 703,000 in 1971. [Ruth S. Callanta, *Poverty: The Philippine Scenario* (Manila: Bookmark, 1988), p. 41.] Between 1957 and 1971, the share of total rural income received by the bottom 40 percent of the people declined from 18 to 13 percent. Over half of that total income went to the richest 20 percent. [William Chapman, *Inside the Philippines Revolution: The New People's Army and its Struggle for Power* (Norton, 1987), p. 91.]

4 Ibid., p. 90.

5 A decade later, when these countries were being cruelly squeezed dry by debt repayments, the banks would be blamed for not having rationed credit more strictly in the 1970s and the borrowing economies blamed for continuing to borrow heavily in the early 1980s—even when it became apparent that the world recession was deepening—and for not taking action to stem capital flight when the crisis supervened. [Donald A. Hay, *Economics Today: A Christian Critique* (Leicester: InterVarsity Press, 1989), p. 267.]

6 Peter Donaldson, *Worlds Apart: The Economic Gulf Between Nations*, Second edition, (Penguin Books, 1986). This book describes the rapid growth in money flowing into the Third World. In 1970 the net flow of (private) resources to underdeveloped countries amounted to US$7 billion dollars. In 1975, it was $25.7 billion and in 1979 it increased to $47.7 billion.

7 Alfonso P. Policarpio, *Ninoy: The Unwilling Martyr* (Quezon City: Isaiah Books, 1986), p. 189.

8 Sandra Burton, *Impossible Dream: The Marcoses, the Aquinos, and the Unfinished Revolution* (New York: Warner Books, 1989), p. 113.

9 *Daily Globe*, 10 September 1991.

Costly Caring

We were becoming bitter over the effects of living out our discipleship. Losing things had come to sum up for us what it meant to be a disciple. We remembered our early days as Christians, when we were continually told that we would receive and gain so much. Reality in the slums made these early promises seem fraudulent.

Some of us in the Servants organization now experienced more pain and suffering than we ever did as non-Christians. We had experienced much hardship in our pre-Christian days because of drugs, occultism and broken families. Yet now our lot seemed far worse. No one had warned us of this when we became Christians.

Many on the Servants Manila team had lost good health at one time or another. One of us, for example, suffered one sickness after another for three years. Some lost a sense of safety. One of our single women was molested three times. Another woman had been confronted by a drunken man while her husband was out. Bellowing at her doorstep, the man demanded to be let in so he could make love to her. Feeling anxious, she refused to respond in any way, other than in prayer. The man abruptly gave up and departed. But the memories remained.

We were also feeling the loss of home comforts. In the midst of humidity, noise, dirt, people and cramped living conditions there was no place to escape. We had no nearby parks to stroll in and enjoy the fresh air. There was no backyard in which we could play with the children, no cool room to retreat to. We had no comfortable chair to sink into and forget about the world.

Life was hard. And it was made harder when the little we did have in terms of material things was taken from us. Rob and Lorraine Ewing returned to their poor community after a day in Manila to discover that literally everything, from toothbrushes to mattresses, had been stolen. All their private mementos from Australia were gone. Psychologically, it was as though they had been violated.

No longer tourists

Pressure was on all of the Servant workers in Manila. The strain of living in these places was taking its toll. The honeymoon was over. We were no longer tourists but residents. Loneliness and exhaustion became our new companions, along with boredom. In our slums every day seemed the same. The humdrum of normality marked our existence—not daily conversions, daring escapades, natural disasters or rescues by angels, all of which seem to feature in many missionary books.

Before leaving for the Philippines most of us in Servants felt we had good rapport with each other. In our small slum houses we found ourselves boxed in by strain and stress. We all drifted into opposite corners. When we most needed each other no one was there to rely on.

We struggled with being confined in such a small physical world. There was little private space. Some found space within themselves and, understandably, others interpreted this as rejection. We were not used to the cramped confines of a slum or our slum houses. In the West most of us either had offices to escape to or a house we could hide in. We even had a beach or a park to escape to. But here we had no way out. We were with people 24 hours a day.

This strain was squeezing our real selves and our real relationships to the surface. Not only were we laboring with the foreign culture, language, climate and the slum context but we also had to contend with ourselves and our relationships.

We had come to Manila with the mandate of incarnation, simplicity, church planting and justice-making. The reality of day-to-day life in a slum made this idea a distant dream. Our letters home spoke not of evangelism and justice but of disillusionment and heartache. From the euphoria of leaving the West and arriving in Manila we were now being swamped by doubts. Had we made the right decision in coming here?

We had come to the end of ourselves. It was no use denying or suppressing what was happening, how we were feeling or what we were thinking. It was time for honesty. With tearful faces we turned to God in prayer but it seemed that he, too, was negative. Instead of hearing comforting words we found ourselves being gently rebuked.

We were being reminded that our joy lay not in our circumstances but in knowing Jesus. Since arriving in our slums we were tempted to believe that if our situation changed then we would be happier. We saw, however, that this category of logic would ultimately demand that we leave the slums because, possibly, our circumstances would never change. We would only find sustaining joy ultimately in communing with Jesus.

Others in Servants were convicted over the issue of "rights"—rights to physical space, a healthy body and uninterrupted sleep. Being released from the need for these rights helped us to discover how much of everything we did in fact have to enjoy.

Most of our team meetings were reduced to tearful sessions, a time to cry without being ashamed. Through our tears we saw more clearly all that was not needed in our lives. Somehow our tears had a healthy dismantling effect. It was as though God was wiping our eyes to help us see who we really were and who we needed to become.

We had come with our idealism, human courage and good intentions, but these were not enough. What we really needed was a revolution in our hearts. To survive, we had no choice but to become a different people, people who could come to terms with this darker side of following Jesus. Oscar Romero, the assassinated Archbishop of San Salvador, has written that "suffering is the shadow of God's hand."[1] We were being called not to think in terms of getting out after three or more years, but to learn what it meant to "remain under" or endure a trial. During that time I read that if we claim the crucified Jesus as our Lord, then it is incumbent upon us to take the pain of the world into ourselves and give it over to Jesus, so that the world may be healed. How long could we last in this attempt?

Many supporters in New Zealand and Australia were lauding us as heroes and modern day saints for how we were living and what we were attempting to do. The irony of this would not have escaped Mary, had she known. We, the missionaries, were considered saints because of the risks we were taking. But Mary and millions of other poor urban dwellers, who for decades had suffered under the burden of their way of life, were not called saints but squatters.

NOTES

1 Oscar Romero, *The Violence of Love: The Pastoral Wisdom of Archbishop Oscar Romero* (San Francisco: Harper & Row, 1988), p. 62.

Mercy Be!

Mary cast her vote for a new Senate and Congress. Not that her vote mattered all that much. By all accounts it was swallowed up in election fraud and massive vote buying.

She wondered if President Cory Aquino could make a difference in a country riddled with corruption. Land reform became the litmus test. The rural and urban sectors desperately needed a just land redistribution program. The homeless and landless peasants waited to see if Aquino's administration would implement such a program. The fact that the President's own family was one of the country's largest landowners did not offer much hope.

Aquino did manage to get a bill passed in Congress promising land reform. But it was a sham, despite the complex legislation that appeared in the statute books. Landowners still held the balance of power in the newly elected legislature and so ensured that there would be enough loopholes in the bill so they could keep their land.

As we surveyed the complexities of Filipino economic life we became more and more insecure about what we were to do in the slums. We felt very uninformed. Language learning, cultural adjustment and survival now seemed quite straightforward compared to the questions, "What do the poor really need?" and "How should we do it?" We lacked experience and expertise in many areas. It was arrogant of us to think that we could come to the Philippines to solve issues of Third World poverty. It has been said that most missionaries, in their ignorance and arrogance, mess things up or become irrelevant. We feared that this could also be our fate.

For most of us this was our first exposure to flesh and blood poverty. This was different from the textbook poverty we had read about from the comfort of our homes in the West. We were shocked by what we saw. It was not right that people were living like this. Something had to be done. And because of our connections with the wealthy West we believed we could do it.

The long lines

The poor started coming to our doors. The ones and twos soon grew into the fifties and hundreds. At times, lines of people greeted us as we opened our doors. These poor had swallowed their pride and come to us hoping for a handout. What do you do when faced with a young mother clutching her dying baby daughter? If we gave, it would become known by all, and the lines would grow longer. If we did not give, the baby might die.

Our hearts ruled the day. We gave to everyone who came. It seemed the only merciful thing to do. Whatever you call it—relief, direct assistance, meeting unmet basic needs, crisis treatment—we did it. We began many mercy ministries, including clothing, medicine, food, housing, schooling and sponsorship.

Just as the Good Samaritan did not look into the background of the dying man he helped on the road, so we also did not ask people to fill out forms or meet certain conditions. We helped everyone, regardless of their circumstances. We expected nothing in return. We believed this was the merciful way of God.

There was a cost to all this mercy. Not all of the money came from the Servants organization, but some came from our own pockets. We had already accepted that as God's servants we were to give sacrificially until our lifestyles were lowered. There was, however, another cost to be paid. We became very tired servants.

The poor kept coming. Each sad story of need was just as tragic as the one before it. Our hearts broke with each account, our minds struggled to understand it and our bodies were burning out from exhaustion. But it was playing God with each and every life that came to our door that really took its toll. It was as though we were dispensing life or death through the decisions we made.

But something was being done. We could see the results: houses for the homeless, food for the hungry, health for the sick and education for the marginalized. It felt good!

Giving loans

If there was to be no genuine wealth redistribution by the elite in the Philippines, then we in Servants would encourage wealth creation through interest-free loans. These loans, we hoped, would create income generating projects or job creation schemes.

It was Monday and we were about to begin another week. The persistent knocking signalled that the week was truly under way. Opening the door with mixed feelings, we saw a distraught mother clutching two children.

"I need to talk with you," she pleaded.

"Come in," we replied. Sitting uncomfortably in the chair she shared her sad familiar story: "My husband has left me. My rent is due. I can't feed the children. Could I ask for a loan to start up a *sari-sari*[1] store?" She was given a form that the local Filipino loan committee had drafted and told that in the coming week she would be visited by her local loan committee representative.

We had to be honest and respect the Filipino-controlled process for giving loans that we had set up some months earlier. Consistency, we had learned, could make the difference between success and failure. "We can't promise you anything," we finally said. Her face, though, continued to communicate that we were her last hope.

"The committee will decide your application," we added.

Standing up to leave, she began to cry. "You're my only hope," she said again. "Thank you, Michael," she said, as she led her children outside.

The following week we all sat down to do business. All the Filipino loan representatives were present with their respective loan application forms. But first, the treasurer reported that we were still hitting the 85 percent loan

Income generation: a *sari-sari* store

repayment rate. This was considered quite a success by other organizations. Some said that the poor were proving to be better at repaying their loans than the middle class.

"We have 20,000 pesos[2] available this month for loans," the treasurer reported. Over the next hour all the applications were discussed, voted on and then prioritized. Four of the six approved applications would be given loans this month and the remaining two next month.

The mother of the two children cried again as she heard that her application had been approved. She gladly signed the contract stating that she had to repay 20 pesos a day until the loan was repaid. A collector would come to her house every afternoon for the money.

She joined about seventy others who had already received such loans. The money had either built or fixed houses, bought medicine or paid hospital bills, bought school clothes and paid fees, started small (micro) income generating businesses and met many other needs. The repaying of the loans gave the poor the sense that they were doing something through their own effort. It also meant that we no longer just gave handouts.

After several months many small enterprises had begun: a piggery; poultry and string making businesses; the selling of fish, milk and shoes; and the setting up of local corner stores. The giving of these loans, interest-free, was also beginning to undermine some of the business of the local loan sharks, who charged crippling interest rates.

The poor were benefitting, which was very satisfying and encouraging. We felt as though we were being merciful as our Father in Heaven was merciful. Interestingly, after Adam and Eve had spurned God, one of the first things God did was to find them some clothes to cover their shame. The acts of God are often acts of mercy.

Jesus' life was also characterized by the meeting of other people's physical needs. So at the end of the day, we felt we were in good company.

Like the story of the Good Samaritan in the Bible, our mercy giving had to be responsive to human need. This meant not just giving medicine, shelter, healing, advocacy or food but actually coming alongside others and offering our physical presence. We learned to be there, "on the road," for others.

As stated earlier, some of us were forever crying out to God, "Where are you on this road of suffering?" God seemed absent in the face of so much pain. And yet we were learning that God could also ask of us, "And where are you on the road?" Were we on the other side of the road, bypassing the needy, as the Priest and Levite did in the story of the Good Samaritan? The scandal is, many Christians are not even "on the road!"

But whom do you help?

One of Mary's sons-in-law asked for a loan to improve his crude plywood hovel. Unfortunately, he used much of the money for his many drinking parties. Some months later he asked for money to buy a refrigerator. Politely, we said we could not help. We felt it was merciful to him, because of his growing addiction to alcohol, to say no. He did not accept this and during a drinking session threatened to shoot us. Nevertheless we persisted with our stand. Saying "no" is never easy.

On the road there are many different types of people: those that deserve assistance and those that are looking to take advantage of big-hearted givers. Under what conditions should we give to the needy on the road? Some Christians press for no conditions. Conditionless mercy, they argue, is the Christian position. Like God, we are to do good for all and love our enemies. We are to give, expecting nothing in return. The poor, they argue, are poor through no fault of their own but because of unfair structures, and must not be held accountable for their situation. If it is not their fault then we should not insist on conditions and the filling out of application papers.

Other equally well-meaning Christians build a case for conditions. We should follow the Pauline injunction to give to those who are truly in need (1 Timothy 5:3-10), and not give to those who may be encouraged to sin because of our giving (1 Timothy 6:9-10). These Christians argue that conditions are necessary because the poor are irresponsible.

We had not really thought all this through as we began our feverish service on behalf of others. This oversight would cost us dearly in the future. But, it seemed, we were finding our place in the vast and overwhelming mass of poverty. We were now no longer just living with the poor, but we were also doing something for the poor. We believed we were doing what we had come to do. And even though we still felt in the dark and lost at sea, slowly that sense of being at home began to surface. Life was looking good. But the fragility of poverty kept us from concluding that things could only get better.

Counting your blessings

Mary's family was quick to avail themselves of the loans and benefit from the mercy ministries. Lea, her daughter, had been taken on as an embroidery worker. Another daughter and her husband were able to buy a house. A son received educational assistance. Mary, however, wanted little of it.

Tony, a Filipino pastor who had been working with us in Damayan Lagi, understood the reason for her reluctance to ask for help or join the missionary's group: pride and self-respect. The missionaries, in her mind, had come with their born again religion and their money. Not surprisingly, the very poor attended the group's meetings in the hope of receiving help. It was not long before the reputation of the missionary's group was set. "That's the group that buys believers," came the charge.

"No self-respecting person would attend their group," concluded Mary. "The moment you step in their door you are known as a 'believer on the take.' That I can do without."

Tony knew us well enough to know that far from wanting to buy believers, we were simply wanting to care for the spiritual and material welfare of the poor. Unfortunately our process communicated the wrong message. Tony could see what was coming.

NOTES

1   A *sari-sari* store is a small store that sells limited quantities of basic items.

2   The exchange rate at the time of publication was approximately 26 pesos to US$1.

The Awful Mistake

Loss, for Ruby and me, was summed up in the death of our third baby, Joseph. Ruby came down with a very sore head while she was pregnant with Joseph. It stayed with her for a few weeks, moving from her head to her stomach. Her regular medical checks raised no alarms so we settled into the calm assurance that everything was all right. God was on our side.

Near the due date, Ruby awoke one morning to find the baby was not moving. We rushed to the hospital, where Ruby was given a caesarean operation. Joseph lived for three weeks. An examination of Ruby's placenta revealed a lot of damage—probably caused by whatever had been causing her headache—depriving Joseph of the oxygen he needed and causing brain damage. We had begun to think that fearful things would not happen to us because we were Christians. This reasoning was taking a real battering.

A few days after the funeral we left the Servants Retreat Center for Damayan Lagi. Walking down the narrow muddy pathway in the slum, Mary met us and asked how the baby was.

"He died," we replied.

"Well, he's an angel now," Mary smiled. "By the way, what are you having for dinner tonight?" We were not shocked that Mary had shifted from death to dinner so easily. For the poor, death is very much a part of life.

Mary, for example, had lost one of her babies, given one away due to her poverty and seen another become a young prostitute. These poor became our healers in the months to come.

When it rains, it pours. Little did we know that the death of Joseph was just the first of many deaths to come. This personal loss was soon followed by much professional loss.

The chickens come home to roost

It was Sunday and I was ready to preach at our fellowship in Damayan Lagi. We had planted this church some months earlier and had quickly outgrown local houses for our meetings. We were now using a local hall. Walking into the hall I quickly checked that everything was in place for the morning's service. While the worship leader led us in prayer, I quickly did a body count. "Not bad," I whispered to Ruby. "About eighty!" Numbers were important to me then. High numbers reassured me that everything was well. Low numbers, though, sent me scrambling for answers and solutions.

I was a product of the church growth movement that had swept through New Zealand during my formative years in the ministry. I believed God wanted a harvest. Expansion was his will. Success was to be measured in terms of numerical growth.

Next to the Bible, my graph book revealed all. Body counts of all descriptions were carefully plotted on the pages: conversions, contacts, recipients of loans and church attendances. Religiously I researched each dot and joining line to discern trends and future projections. I was a graph man.

After the sermon I closed the service with prayer. At home, Ruby and I did our regular postmortem of the service. We were worried. We had sung the praise songs but it seemed there was little worship. I felt I had been preaching to myself. There was no sense of involvement in the service. We were going through the motions, doing what was expected, adhering to form. But despite the encouraging numbers, we had a conviction that all was not well.

"What really is happening in our fellowship?" we asked the more mature believers the following week. "We are worried. It seems that we're pretending to be church." Honesty has a way of begetting honesty in others.

"The problem," they each replied, "is that only a few are genuine Christians."

"But how can that be?" we pleaded, remembering all the hours of prayer and Bible study that we had poured into leading people to Christ.

"It's *utang na loob* [the obligation to return a favor]."

A bit on the defensive, we asked what they meant.

"Many come to your religious groups because they simply want to return the favor that you did for them with your mercy giving and loans."

We began to understand. We had met their needs so now they were doing something significant for us. Our friendship and their church attendance had been reduced to a simple transaction. We had given help, and so as rich Westerners had stuck to our side of the unwritten deal. For their part, they would attend our services while they were still paying off the loans. Everyone was happy. Their cupboards weren't so bare and my graphs were up.

"But we want people to come to Christ through faith and repentance, not because of money and favors," I argued with Ruby. "We didn't come all this way to live in slums just to establish groups of rice Christians!"[1]

Stop it all!

"So what do we do?" we asked those we had been helping.

"Stop all the loans and mercy ministries!"

We could not believe what we were hearing. These were poor folk who were blocked from getting credit from the middle class banks in Manila. Their only recourse, apart from our schemes, were the loan sharks with their exorbitant interest rates. Our loan program provided a way of getting credit with no interest. And yet they were now asking us to close it down.

They proceeded to share with us that the loan program was creating more harm than good. Not only was it creating a mass of rice Christians but it was also bringing about communal breakdown. The very fact that we had to choose one person over another when giving loans was leading to misunderstanding, jealousy and strained relationships in the community. In other words, the social cost of all our giving was too high. Even though they were poor, these people preferred relational harmony over material gain.

We learned another lesson. In our evangelical earnestness we had come out as the teachers ready to impart all. Now we were becoming the students and the people we had come to help were the teachers. The teacher in us was being tamed by our own ignorance and arrogance, and by their wisdom.

Figure 5.1: Ministries before and after 1988

Ministries Before 1988	Ministries After 1988
Mercy ministry	Stopped
Income generation schemes	Stopped
Loan facility	Stopped
Medical care	Stopped
Emergency Relief	Stopped
80-100 member church	20 member church

We phased out most of what we had begun (see Figure 5.1 on page 41). Over the next month my graphs took some sharp downward turns. From a church attendance of 80 we went down to 25. Closing down the loan program separated the genuine believers from the rice Christians.

A theology of failure

But the pain we felt was real. Months of hard work was now rendered suspect. Some of us felt like failures. We had believed, prayed and even fasted over the years. We had poured our lives into the work. Yet despite all of this, the work was now crumbling around us.

These feelings of failure were not helped when we got letters from home responding to a paper that we had sent to some people. It was important for our supporters to read the paper to keep them informed of our journey. Too often missionaries write home and tell only of the successes, the good side. We wanted to be honest. We took a risk and shared about the darker side of our ministry, and confessed to making mistakes. We needed to hear words of acceptance and encouragement. Yet some of the letters came close to condemning us. "Why," they charged, "didn't you realize this in the beginning? Why did it take so long to recognize the error of your ways? Why the sudden revision?"

These questions put us on the defensive. How could they judge us when they lived in a different part of the world where the social system in which we lived was unknown to them? We, and not they, were caught up in the complex world of fragile poverty. In such a context one could not expect anything else but a fragile ministry.

We were hurt. Somehow we had to understand what it meant to be a failure. As for being open and forthcoming about our mistakes and failures, it is something we will continue to do. As J. Andrew Kirk writes:

Paradoxically, one of the greatest strengths of Christian faith is its ability to deal creatively and confidently with abject failures. In principle, at least, those who seek to live after the pattern of Jesus Christ have no need for pretence. They are free to admit mistakes and absurdities. There is no particular reason, apart from a normal human tendency in this direction, why they should need to justify the error of their ways. Never are Christians more faithful to the message they say they believe than when they admit their frequent faults.[2]

Some members of the Servants team were not in agreement with this. They admitted that some mistakes were made, but "failure" was too strong a word to describe all that had happened. As Christians, they argued, could we ever say anything was a failure? Surely, they pressed, God redeems all and so nothing in the end could be considered a failure. They reminded us of the scriptural promise:

> *And we know that in all things God works for the good of those who love him, who have been called according to his purpose (Romans 8:28).*

Paul, a failure?

The apostle Paul used the term "failure" when evaluating his own work (1 Thessalonians 2:1). And Paul definitely endured failure in his own ministry. Interestingly, Paul gives us no record of his first sixteen years in ministry. These were years spent in Arabia, Damascus, Syria and Cilicia (Acts 9:19-25, 1 Thessalonians 2:14-16, Galatians 1:21, Acts 11:25). We are not told of any lasting results from these years. Did Paul then suffer from many wilderness years, as we were now experiencing?

Furthermore, Paul failed to unite the Jewish and Gentile Christians (Galatians 2:11-13). He failed to resolve the difficulties he had with Barnabas (Acts 15:36-41) which ultimately resulted in the rupture of their friendship. The church at Corinth, where Paul spent much of his time, proved to be very difficult and sinful. Often he wondered whether his labor had been in vain.

In terms of economic projects, Paul's record is dubious. In the closing years of his ministry he devoted much of his time to collecting from the Gentiles a fund for the poor in Jerusalem (Galatians 2:10). His collection effort often proved disastrous and when he got to Jerusalem we are not told what happened to the money. This other side of Paul encouraged us.

Joseph, a failure?

Joseph of the Old Testament also encouraged us. Admittedly, his initial interpretation of Pharaoh's dreams and the subsequent collection of food was impressive. But what started out as good turned bad. Joseph ended up destroying the purchasing power of the people by taking away all their money (Genesis 47:14-15), the cattle and flocks that were their means of livelihood and work (47:16-17), and their land and gave it all to Pharaoh (47:20-21).

Joseph's economic project ended with people having no money, no livestock and no land. Tragically, Joseph's actions set the stage for the enslavement of his people. One theologian comments that "the conditions of slavery that the children of Israel were to suffer were prepared by a son of Israel."[3] What kind of success is that?

Most of the key players in Scripture are depicted as men and women with feet of clay. Theirs is a journey of faithfulness and failure with little success. Yet our own modern Christian heritage has promised us something else. We are told that we can reach our goals, maximize our potential, believe for miracles and know how to be successful. We have been taught a gospel of success.

"What we need to do," I shared with Colin Harrington, our international leader at the time, "is construct a theology of failure or a theological framework for working through failure." Somewhat despondent, we sat on a dirty log on one of the muddy pathways in Damayan Lagi and wondered what this would mean. We needed to have a theological framework that would embrace weakness, disappointments, making mistakes and failure.

"Despite all that has happened, all the mistakes and failure, God is still pleased that at least some of his people are with the poor of the earth," we finally concluded. "He is still smiling on us!"

A crisis of faith

Over the coming months I sagged into a crisis of faith (see Figure 5.2 on page 46). We had stopped many of our programs, our churches dwindled in numbers, missionaries were leaving and some of our prized converts were falling away. It was all coming apart.

It seemed that being a believer in Christ made no difference at all. Faith, prayer, clean living and hard work counted for little. In the face of poverty all of these were rendered ineffective and powerless. I was losing certainty about God, Jesus Christ and the Holy Spirit. Right and wrong, good and bad began to blur. I began to doubt whether there was a place any more for Christian virtues, godly disciplines and spirituality.

I had read of how social workers, missionaries, pastors and priests who had immersed themselves among the poor had ended up disillusioned cripples clutching a bottle, hoping to escape the memories of their failures. I now understood how this could happen. I began to drink. Not only that, but one night I came very close to doing something very stupid with an attractive neighbor of ours. I was not coping too well. The losses of the past four years

Figure 5.2: The results of a crisis of faith

Crisis of Faith

Dogmaticism   Revisionism   Reactionism

Resentment   Reconversion   Cynical
                                          Withdrawal

were beginning to catch up with me: the loss of New
Zealand; the loss of comfort, security and health; the loss
of Joseph, of the loan scheme and many of the believers
in Damayan Lagi; the loss of fellow workers and missionaries; and finally, the loss of faith and self-respect.

"How loss affects you," writes Michael Riddell,
"depends upon your relation to that which is lost. When
you have loved what you lose, a part of you goes with it."[4]
But, as Riddell then writes:

> The dark days are just beginning. Before you
> emerge into the light again you will be stripped to
> the core. You will rage and scream at God. You will
> retreat into a cocoon of sorrow and breathe in slow
> motion. The colour will drain from the sky, the
> meaning from life. As a plough tears through hard
> earth, your heart will be broken up. You will make
> friends with pain, nursing it as the child of grief.
> Utter emptiness fills the earth, and the valley
> appears to contain nothing but the echo of your

own cry. Surely God has left you. The road which seemed to be heading somewhere has become a dead end. A mocking maze with no exit.

Then, one morning in the distant future, you wake and hear a bird singing . . .[5]

For now, the bird was not singing. I was utterly distraught. Three years of blood, sweat and tears, reduced to a cry of "STOP IT ALL!" I was not prepared for this. It was not what I had expected or had been led to believe would happen.

I was now in the throes of unbelief. It is said by some that we all go through various stages of faith (see Figure 5.3 on page 48). Initially, we imitate those who are strong in the faith. Then we become strong ourselves by owning our own convictions and beliefs. We then move on and attempt to relate these convictions to the world around us. But it is the fourth stage, where we come face to face with a crisis, that brings into question much of what we have believed. Invariably we respond in one of three ways to this crisis.

Some of us dig our heels in. In other words, even though we suspect that what we have believed thus far has been found wanting in some respects, we choose to ignore this and stubbornly believe what we always have, even though we know it is lacking. This response invariably ends up in resentment.

The second response is that of cynical withdrawal. Our faith has not worked out so there is no other option but to discard it all, "to throw the baby out with the bath water" and to become bitter. I was tempted to do this.

But there is another way out—a third response. I was to learn this through a quite unexpected departure from Damayan Lagi.

Figure 5.3: James Fowler's stages of faith[6]

▶ **Stage 1: Intuitive-Projective Faith**

Imitative phase where we are powerfully influenced by the example, actions and stories of others. An episodic phase.

▶ **Stage 2: Mythic-Literal Faith**

Where we begin to take on for ourselves stories, beliefs and observations. Beliefs are appropriated with literal interpretations, as are moral rules and attitudes. Symbols are taken as literal in meaning.

▶ **Stage 3. Synthetic-Conventional Faith**

A number of spheres demand attention: family, school or work, peers, street society and so on. Faith must provide a coherent orientation in the midst of this more complex and diverse range of involvements. In a sense it is a conformist stage. However, this phase also sets in motion factors that may contribute to the breakdown of this faith: serious clashes, contradictions between valued authority sources, marked changes, encounters with experiences that demand a critical reflection on one's faith, leaving home and so on.

▶ **Stage 4: Individuative-Reflective Faith**

Where the adult must begin to take seriously the burden of responsibility for his or her own commitments, lifestyle, beliefs and attitudes. The self that was sustained in its identity within the circle of significant others now claims an identity no longer defined by that circle.

This is a "demythologizing" stage. It has to do with its capacity for critical reflection on identity and ideology. A time of disturbing inner voices, disillusionment and recognition that life is more complex than previously thought. A move toward a more dialectical approach to truth.

▶ **Stage 5. Conjunctive Faith**

The integration of self and outlook of much that was suppressed or unrecognized in the interest of Stage 2's self-certainty. Here there is a new reclaiming and reworking of one's past. There must be an opening to the voices of one's "deeper self." This stage is alive to paradox and the truth in apparent contradictions. It strives to unite opposites in mind and experience. It is ready for closeness to that which is different and threatening to self and outlook.

The strength of this stage is the ability to be in one's own group but recognizing that it is relative, partial and distorted. Its danger is that it can give rise to passivity, inaction, complacency or cynical withdrawal.

◗ Stage 6. Universalizing Faith

A new and more comprehensive vision of the truth, inclusive and making real in a tangible way (the activist incarnation) of the partial apprehensions seen in stage 5. Persons in this stage usually exhibit qualities that shake our usual criteria of normalcy. Their heedlessness to self-preservation and their devotion to universalizing compassion that may offend our parochial perceptions of justice threaten our measured standards of goodness. Persons in this stage have the quality of redemptive subversiveness. They have visions to which they have committed their total beings. They are visions born out of radical acts of identification with persons and circumstances where the futurity of being is crushed, blocked or exploited.

NOTES

1 Rice Christians: People who become Christian to get some material benefit.

2 J. Andrew Kirk, *Loosing the Chains: Religion as Opium and Liberation* (Hodder & Stoughton, 1992), p. 122.

3 M. Douglas Meeks, *God the Economist: The Doctrine of God and Political Economy* (Minneapolis: Fortress Press, 1989), p. 79.

4 Michael Riddell, *Godzone: A Traveller's Guide* (Oxford: Lion, 1992), pp. 42-43.

5 Ibid., p. 43.

6 James W. Fowler, *Stages of Faith: The Psychology of Human Development and the Quest for Meaning* (New York: Harper & Row, 1981), pp. 122-211.

A Revolution from the Heart

One night I awoke with a nagging question: Why are you here in the Philippines? The answer seemed obvious: We were here to serve the poor, to be servants.

Then another voice entered the discussion. I sensed God speaking to me. "You are here," I felt he was saying, "not just to do things *for* the poor, but also to work *with* the poor." For the rest of the night I grappled with what that meant. A week later I was introduced to a book that was to bring about a revolution in our hearts.

The book was the story of Father Niall O'Brien, a Catholic missionary priest and member of the Society of St. Columban. Father O'Brien had lived and worked with the very poor of Negros, in the Philippines, for over twenty years. His encounters with widespread injustice, political corruption, crushing poverty, illegal arrests and torture led to his arrest and imprisonment under Marcos, on a phoney charge of murder.

O'Brien helped the poor to help themselves. He had created self-reliant communities where the poor prayed together, looked after one another, cared for their own sick and dying, gained courage from Scripture and worked for political action.[1] Page after page presented a powerful message: it is better to work *with* the poor than do things *for* the poor.

As we surveyed our first four years in the Philippines we concluded that Servants had done much *for* the poor.

We had given food, bandaged the sick, built houses, created jobs, made converts and constructed churches. Like some corporate Santa Claus we had spread abroad many gifts. Not surprisingly, one of our number referred to us all as "the walking wallets" in the slums.

But we had done little *with* the poor. O'Brien's book raised many questions that challenged our efforts. Had we taken the time to see what the poor could give? In our giving, had we robbed the poor of their opportunity to sacrificially give to one another? Had we unintentionally communicated to the poor that what they had did not count, that foreign was better than domestic? Had we done things for them that they could have done for themselves? Had we ended up controlling their destiny? Put simply, had we disempowered them?

What had our giving done to us as missionaries? One woman in Servants had struggled with playing god with the poor. She had the power to give and radically transform a poor family, but she also had the power to withhold help. She could control the destiny of people's lives. Living with this responsibility became too much and was one of the reasons for her departure. "I can't be God to these people!" she exclaimed.

Furthermore, our giving seemed to compromise our precious incarnational mandate. We had relocated into the heart of the slums so as to be one with the people, but our giving had made us the elite of the slum, the patrons, the upper class. As the providers we were now the benefactors and the poor were the beneficiaries.

The school

It was back to the drawing board. The mistakes, failures and crises of faith forced us to review what we had done. We needed to learn lessons. Most of us had experienced pain on the streets; now we were to discover pain in the study. The books we read showed us we were on the right learning track.

- ❖ We discovered that we should not seek to do for others what they must do for themselves.
- ❖ Many skills are either already present or can be produced within the people.
- ❖ We should not focus so much on designing programs "on behalf of others." Rather, we should strive to collaborate with others in developing the emotional and practical resources they require.
- ❖ Enhance the possibilities for people to control their own lives.
- ❖ Foster local initiatives.
- ❖ The people should participate in their own development.

Although some of these concepts were new to us we discovered that the key thoughts were thousands of years old. Lao Tsu penned these words in 700 B.C.:

Go to the people, live with them,
  learn from them, love them.
Start with what they know,
  build on what they have.
But with the best leaders when the work is done,
  and the task is accomplished,
The people will say,
  We have done this ourselves.[2]

"Go to the people." We had done that. "Live with them." We had done that. "Love them." Well, we had tried. But "learn from them, start with what they know and build on what they have?" These we had not done. When we arrived in Damayan Lagi we took one look at the slum and its inhabitants and concluded they were in a desperate plight. As far as we were concerned, there was nothing good there. This was our first mistake. We concluded that the people had nothing to offer and it was up to us to do all we could. Thus began the array of mercy-giving options, job creation schemes and capital loan facilities.

We were now being asked to believe that in the midst of the muddy and disease-ridden pathways, the crude, ramshackle houses, the open sewers and cramped conditions, there were numerous resources. We could add what we had to offer to these resources, but we had to get the starting point right and not create the perception that *our* resources were the most important.

A new identity

We had already made the mistakes. We knew it and so did everyone else. It was humbling walking the streets. All we wanted to do was escape the slum and start afresh somewhere else with our new ideas. We no longer had respect. We were no longer the experts, teachers and saviors to be looked up to, to be eagerly listened to and followed. We felt like children.

As we read we realized this should have been our attitude from the beginning. We should have come as fellow travellers, as children not as adults, as learners not as teachers, in weakness not strength. We should have come willing to share our flawed humanity with the poor as a sign of solidarity with them. We were not to discount the place of the expert, teacher and healer but to complement them with weakness, fragility, openness and vulnerability. Often, showing our weaknesses can accomplish more than merely depending upon our strengths.

A new partnership

"That is all well and good," complained one of the Servant missionaries, "but where do I now fit in the scheme of things? Do I have a place any more? If it's all up to the people why not just go home?" We were in danger of ending up with a high view of the poor person and a low view of the missionary, empowering the poor and demoralizing the Servant worker. "If the Servant worker comes off second best in all of this rethinking," we responded, "then it's only because we are trying to correct the imbalance." For so long the poor person had been demoralized in the development process led by foreigners and national experts. But in lifting the poor up we were not wanting to then demean the role of the missionary.

A new formula was taking shape. The poor were to do all that they could do and only then would we do *with* them what they could not do by themselves. By doing everything for them, we were robbing the poor of their opportunity to help each other. Thus we were also robbing them of the joy there is in laying one's life down for a friend.

We would have to wait and see if and how these new ideas would work, but they felt right. Development was to be a shared process that respected both the dignity of the poor and the missionary.

A new criticism

It was important to share the debates and all that we were learning with our supporters in New Zealand and elsewhere. We carefully documented and explained our thoughts. Some months later one of the Servant workers said that his pastor had read some of our new thinking and charged us with becoming liberal, left wing and a danger to Christendom.

We were a bit concerned about the first two labels. We were tempted to take the charge of being a danger to Christendom as a compliment. The church is in desper-

Figure 6.1: Your theological journey

After reading the following brief definitions of each theology, plot your own journey in theology. For example, name the theology you started with and state why you started there. Then state the theology you may have changed to and give a reason for the change. Finally, state the theology that best describes where you are now or where you would like to be.

The Theologies

❖ **Humanization Theology**: Social action is the only agenda. No evangelism. What matters is making the world a better place–and nothing else.

❖ **Liberation Theology**: Social action is the priority but there is a place for evangelism.

❖ **Salvation Theology**: The salvation of souls is the only priority. There is no place for social action.

❖ **Evangelization Theology**: Salvation of souls is the priority but there is a place for social action.

❖ **Transformation Theology**: Evangelism and social action are distinct priorities but are of equal importance.

ate need of "denial ideas" and rebels, those who challenge the status quo. On the charge of being a liberal, the pastor felt that by suggesting that we should now learn from the poor and that the poor could do much in their own transformation, we were ending up with such a high view of the poor person that we were contradicting his view of the Bible's picture of the human person as utterly depraved.

At first glance the Bible does appear to have a negative view of the human person: "The Lord saw how great man's wickedness on the earth had become, and that every inclination of the thoughts of his heart was only evil all the time" (Genesis 6:5).

This verse is not a very positive starting point for those involved in community development. The Bible, however, often holds two things in tension. On the one hand, there is a picture of our twisted egos and selfishness. But on the other hand, there is also the picture of being made in the image of God and endowed with natural abilities, talents and competencies.

As Christians we need to remember that the unredeemed person is still made in the image of God and so must not be dehumanized. Humankind is unworthy before God but that does not make a person worthless. Christians have much to learn at the hands of unbelievers and, at times, it will be the unredeemed who will preach to and rebuke the Lord's people (Genesis 12:18-20, 20:8-13).

A new priority

We returned to our slums with heads buzzing with new insights and ideas. We were still faced with the thousands of urban poor. Despite all that we had learned we were plagued with the question, "Where do we start?"

Aid organizations encouraged us to start by meeting the physical needs of the people. Churches told us to begin with the preaching of Jesus Christ. Left wing non-government organizations urged us to join them and protest against injustice. We wanted to do all of these and more. But which should come first? What was to be our priority?

We had often grappled with these questions. For example, one of our Servant workers had clearly stated her position: "I came out here to get people to heaven!" The response came: "It's all very well people enjoying life after death, but what about life before death?"

Often the projects focused the debate. One group in the slum asked for assistance to build a public toilet; they had done all they could but needed some extra capital.

"Should we help?" we asked ourselves.

"The area has no Christian witness," someone responded, "and so helping with this project will soften the hearts of the people to our message."

A silence came over the room. We knew something was not right here. Doing projects to get people to listen raised all sorts of questions for some of us. When helping others should we expect anything in return, even the conversion of others? Jesus obviously thought not (Luke 6:35).

"But without a religious dimension," the debate went on, "is there still any value in building a toilet?"

"But can't toilets be valuable just because they are meeting a need?" replied another. "Does it have to be a 'Christian' toilet to be valuable?"

"Aren't we in danger of becoming just another well-meaning group that works hard at making this world a better place for people to live in, but loses sight of the world to come?"

"Well at least we can pray about the toilet," offered one of our regular peacemakers. This thought was revolutionary. So often we had prayed for people to come to Christ, or for churches and their pastors. To now pray for guidance over a toilet was a radical shift in focus. Something seemed right about the idea. God was not "out to lunch" when projects and material matters were concerned.

Finally we understood: our study and experience encouraged us to start with the people. Community life would determine the priority at any given time. The Bible seemed to place the people as its priority. Deliverance from sin, demons, physical hardships and injustice are all of equal concern. God is pro life—life before and after death! The needs of others would, by and large, dictate which of these we should do at any given time. We see this in the pattern of Jesus' life. Sometimes he spoke first, while at other times he acted first.

Figure 6.2: Models of evangelism

	Anthropology	Sin	Content of Gospel	Meaning of Salvation
Model One: **Individualistic** **Evangelical**	People are isolated individuals, rather than persons in community–strong body-soul dichotomy	Emphasis is on personal sins like lying and adultery	Salvation of individual	Justification and regeneration of individuals
Model Two: **Radical** **Anabaptist**	People are both individuals personally responsible to God and persons in community	Some emphasis on social sin but main emphasis is on personal sin	Good News of the kingdom	Both justification and regeneration of individuals and the new redeemed community of the church
Model Three: **Dominant** **Ecumenical**	A balance of personal and communal	Personal and social but for many the emphasis falls heavily on the social	Good News of the kingdom	• Justification and regeneration of individuals • Church • Increasing peace and justice in society outside the church is also salvation (for some, this receives greatest emphasis)
Model Four: **Secular** **Christian**	Personal and communal	Offense against neighbor and structural injustice	Good News about the possibility of social progress	Good News about the possibility of social progress

This was scary stuff! For some of us, praying for deliverance over demons was easier than marching with people on the streets. For others, working at projects for deliverance over physical hardships was easier than personal evangelism. But to be willing to do all of these demanded of us a courage to become the kind of people we had never been before.

Furthermore, we would have to break out of our Servants enclave and learn from others. We would go to the

and social action[3]

History and Eschatology	Source of Theological Truth	Object of Evangelism	How is Gospel Shared?	How is Society Changed?	Locus of God's Activity
Little continuity	Bible	Only persons	Largely proclamation of Word	As converted individuals are salt and light	Primarily the church (all saving activity occurs there)
Little continuity	Bible	Only persons	Both word and deed (visible demonstration of common life of Jesus' new redeemed community, the church		Primarily the church (all saving activity occurs there)
Great continuity (in liberal version, there is little emphasis on Christ's return)	Bble, reason, tradition, human experience (especially each local context)	Persons and social structures	Word and deed (includes both life of church and political action in society)	Through conversation, life of the church, restructuring social institutions (in liberal version, last is most important)	God's redeeming activity occurs in both the church and the world
History is the only reality	Reason and human experience are decisive	Only social structures	The Gospel of Social Progress is shared via politics	Only through restructuring society	Only the world

Catholics to learn about solidarity with the poor. We would go to the Pentecostals to learn about the Holy Spirit. We would go to the Baptists to learn about preaching the gospel and we would go to the liberals to learn about fighting for social justice. Our engagement with the poor was encouraging us to be more ecumenical, to be more representative of the breadth of ministry of the body of Christ.

Manila to Oxford

"You have got to get out!" the team pleaded with Ruby and me. "Take a furlough and get away from here for a while." They could see that the whole crisis had taken a lot out of us. We were tired, intense and discouraged.

"But we can't," we replied. "We have just begun to learn some key lessons. It's time to work them out in practice. We just can't drop things like that."

Our colleagues withdrew and had a meeting without us. Colin Harrington was in town at the time so they consulted him. Later that afternoon they returned and gave us the word: "Go!"

Under this kind of pressure we felt we had to submit to the team. Some months earlier I had noticed an advertisement on the back of a magazine. It was for a course in Oxford, England, for Christian practitioners who had spent time among the poor and needed to do some critical reflection. At the time, I had told Ruby that we should go there for our upcoming furlough. She needed little persuading.

Going to England seemed like a dream come true. Within 24 hours of leaving Damayan Lagi we were in Oxford. My first impression was that this place must be heaven. Tidy little streets, beautiful spacious parks, friendly pubs on every corner and most importantly, book shops and libraries making available the wisdom of the ages.

NOTES

1   Niall O'Brien, *A Revolution from the Heart* (New York: Oxford Press, 1987).

2   Anne Hope et. al., *Training for Transformation*, Book 1 (Gweru: Mambo Press, 1984), p. 82.

3   Ronald Sider, *Evangelism and Social Action* (London: Hodder & Stoughton, 1993), pp. 26-27.

Thinkers at the Coal Face

Our engagement so far had been with flesh and blood poverty and not with textbook or "armchair" poverty. As practitioners we had sought to "walk the walk" and not just "talk the talk."

I emphasize this point because talking about poverty has become very fashionable. Social concern and all its related cousins is now a popular growth industry among Christians. This has generated a much needed verbal advocacy on behalf of the poor and needy. This is what I call textbook or armchair poverty. There is a need for Christians to think about the issues.

But is a corresponding incarnational advocacy also growing, where Christians actually live, struggle and sacrifice with those on whose behalf they so eloquently speak? Far from wanting to demean those who talk about poverty, I wish to see more Christians prepared to share with the poor—where the poor are and in what they are doing.

Jesus' advocacy was a bodily one (Hebrews 10:5,10) and not just one of mental concern. His knowledge of the poor was subjective and not just abstract. We read of Jesus being found with the poor much more than in the debating chamber discussing their situation. It was partly in imitation of this Jesus that we were encouraged to leave the comforts of our homes and relocate to the slums of the Third World.

But we had done enough walking and it was now time to talk. We had made too many mistakes, at much cost to ourselves and to the poor. We needed to share these mistakes with other workers so that we could reflect together.

We had gone to the shanties of Manila in the mold of many evangelicals of that time. We went with hearts full of compassion and an earnestness to do the Father's will– to obey, no matter what the sacrifice. We had cultivated the heart and the will, but we had left the mind uncultivated. We struggled to love the Lord with our strength and souls, but not so much with our minds. In our haste to be involved we forgot to think critically. This neglect affected our mission in the slums in five ways.

1   We plunged into mission unthinkingly. We had at our disposal an array of missiological keys. These, we were told, would usher in the kingdom. So in a somewhat lurching fashion we swung from one key to another. If one proved ineffective then we tried another. Looking back, a more informed theological framework or grid would have helped us to sift these keys. Pausing to reflect on our theology would probably have removed much of the lurching.

2   "Gut compassion" was the rule of the day. The cries of our own hearts and the cries of the poor dictated our actions. Such compelling compassion is needful but, by itself, insufficient. We also needed "critical compassion" to guide our actions–critical in the sense that in serving the poor our minds must also be engaged, not just our hearts. With our minds we seek to discern the most appropriate way to serve the poor, the way that will result in genuine empowerment and not disempowerment. It is one thing to react to the horrors of poverty and act in unthinking

ways but quite another to intelligently interact with this world and help its people appropriately.

3 In the absence of a more informed theological grid to sift our decisions, we ended up using other grids. We gave way to legalism (use what has been tried before), pragmatism (use what works and can be managed), subjectivism (each worker should respond to their own attitude and preference), relativism (only listen to the Filipino–this is where we are), and utilitarianism (what is the most useful). We did not use all of these simultaneously, but inevitably some team members wanted to apply one "ism" while others were of a different persuasion.

As you can imagine, with each person influenced by their own respective "ism" our team discussions and policymaking meetings were marked by diversity and therefore, at times, frustration and tension. And given the breadth of Scripture, each could come up with a proof text supporting their particular "ism."

4 Without a theological grid we were also in danger of allowing the social sciences to reign. In other words, we were in danger of using the Scriptures for our personal discipleship but using the social sciences for our professional work. The insights of anthropology, sociology and the like were proving extremely helpful for some. To admit to this was one thing, but to submit to these disciplines in an uncritical fashion was another.

5 In the absence of a well-defined theological framework we were in danger of de-emphasizing theology altogether, and of being driven by what was necessary, expedient and manageable.

We found ourselves in a vicious cycle. Without a theological grid we came under the influence of other taskmasters and these new masters, be they the family of "isms," the social sciences or management theory, undermined and demeaned theology.

As Christians we knew it was meant to be the other way around. Instead of all the "isms" and sciences critiquing and reducing theology, the latter should question and indeed challenge the former. We did not know how to do this. We had no defined theological framework in place that could help us to critically discern—not dismiss—all that the "isms" and sciences had to say about the poor and how to effectively empower them.

Oxford Centre for Mission Studies

Oxford was the place for us to be nurtured "in the armchair." We studied at the Oxford Centre for Mission Studies (OCMS)[1] under the direction of Dr. Christopher (Chris) Sugden. Chris sought to integrate Third World development studies with other academic disciplines. We also did some post-graduate work in theology and ethics at Oxford University. This required several months of residential study as well as sitting the Oxford exams. We also had to write a number of theses and long essays, but we could do these from the mission field.

While in Europe I told our story at many churches and conventions. After speaking people often asked me why an experienced missionary to the poor was also studying at a place like Oxford. They found it difficult to reconcile the two. The journey in the slums represented "hands on" ministry, while Oxford conjured up images of ivory tower scholarly irrelevancy far removed from the realities of Third World poverty. How wrong they were!

Theology and development

Our particular course at the OCMS was advertised as a post-graduate course in theology and development studies. Some of my colleagues could understand going to the United Kingdom to study development issues, but theology was something else. My study of theology at Oxford–biblical, systematic, philosophical or liberation theology–surprised even me. They enriched my understanding of our involvement in mission. Far from being irrelevant, these theologies provided me with tools to better assess what we were doing on the streets in the slums of Asia.

At first I too refused to believe that theology was the way to go. I had come to reflect on development issues, not theology. During our first term I appreciated the input by development practitioners that Chris brought to the Centre, but considered the theology lectures at Oxford University to be a waste of time. In our second term, however, I began to think differently. I found myself using the theology to biblically critique what the development practitioners were saying.

Systematic theology, for example, gave me a thematic framework for working through issues. This framework or grid helped me systematically and thematically sift all that we faced on the streets. The themes were of creation and redemption, personal and social sin, life before and after death, the kingdom now and later, the human as sinner and in the image of God and so on. Thus, when exploring a particular problem I saw how it was necessary to probe all of these themes to see how they contributed to the picture.

Biblical theology, on the other hand, kept me faithful to the whole of Scripture. At Oxford I was encouraged to see the Bible as a story that has a beginning, a middle and an end. When facing an issue in the world, it is not a matter of plucking out a few proof texts to try and put that issue in perspective. That hardly does justice to the complexity on the streets. Rather, we must bring each issue into the light of each of the main phases of the Bible's story.[2] The phases include the Creation, the Fall, Israel as a community, Israel in disintegration, Jesus, the new Israel and the future.

Allowing the whole sweep of biblical narrative to inform us keeps us from making the same mistake as some liberation theologians, who sift everything through only one phase–the Exodus event. It also saves us from making the error that some evangelical church growth devotees tend to make when they limit themselves to the specifics of Paul's teachings, neglecting the prophetic contributions of Jesus, Amos and others. Instead, the witness of the whole Bible must inform each issue we face. But first we must spend time studying the many historical phases and identifying various themes of Scripture to know how to best use them when interacting with street life.

Philosophical theology frightens us, but it need not. This theology helped us to clarify and reflect critically on what we see as truth. As a result we often identified parts of our thinking that were inconsistent. In other words, OCMS did not give us a package of knowledge to regurgitate at the end of the year. Rather, it equipped us to examine our approach to knowledge. We were not to use clichés, half-truths, slogans or unquestioned assumptions. Sadly, many Christians use these in their defence of truth. I came away from Oxford feeling as though I had undergone rigorous mental exercise, and having a better idea of what counts as a valid argument and what does not. It was very humbling.

Liberation theology reminded us of the importance of doing for correct understanding, that right action is just as important as right belief. Because most of us were practitioners, we liked this emphasis.

The study of these theologies helped us become lateral thinkers–to use more than one discipline to dig for knowledge and understanding. This has opened up new reservoirs and more creative thinking. David Cook, one of my tutors and author of the helpful book, *The Moral Maze*, underlines this when he comments on the lateral thinking advocated by Edward de Bono:

> He [de Bono] complained that most of our attempts to teach people to think were along vertical lines. We taught people to dig the same hole deeper. Hence the move to increasing specialisation and more and more knowledge about less and less. He introduced lateral thinking, which is a formalised name for what many of us do naturally. If one hole doesn't look as if it will produce oil, we drill other holes in likely spots. In other words, we move sideways to try and see the problem in a different light and try a new approach.[3]

A community of learners

At times the OCMS resembled a global village or railway station. There were visitors and students from Uganda, South Africa, Mexico, Bosnia and many other countries. We became a community of learners. I was not permitted simply to absorb it all, retreat and then regurgitate everything I had learned. Far from being a private affair, study became a communal experience. We sifted ideas through a communal grid; we learned to do theology in community. But more significantly, this continual cross-cultural exposure critiqued much of what I had come to understand as the gospel of Jesus Christ.

We also interacted on a regular basis with highly reputable Christian scholars who helped us make the connection between scholarly study and ministry in our particular contexts. Furthermore, the program left ample time for reflection. Time was given to withdraw and process what had been given. I learned to critically

Figure 7.1: The approaches to decision-making[4]

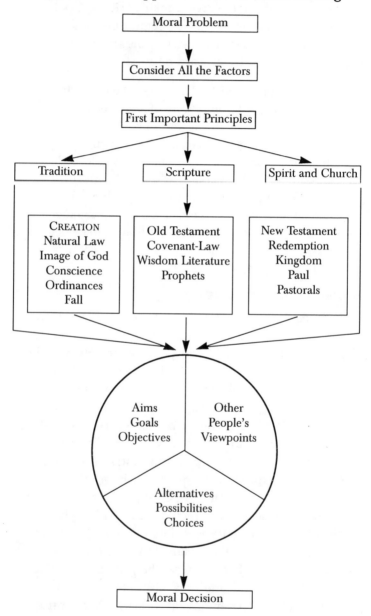

"unpack" and rework ideas so I could give my own contribution to the debate. We were constantly pressed to share what we thought. This process developed contemplative and debating skills.

It was not just a "head" affair at OCMS. I studied with my peers; we had all done time among the world's poor and were of similar age and experience. In this context, one's thinking is challenged the most. But we grow the most when we are threatened the most. So while I was at the OCMS personal transformation also occurred. The team that I worked with in Manila have often remarked that I came back a different person.

Conclusion

Before Oxford, I thought it was only the practitioner that suffered pain. At Oxford, however, I experienced the very real pain of sitting in the armchair. Grappling with issues and attempting to work out solutions demanded perseverance, brutal honesty and humility. Whether on the streets or in the study, a painful journey unfolds. But it is in embracing the pain that we can make a new beginning. My time at the Oxford Centre for Mission Studies gave me a new beginning in mission.

The French sociologist, Jacques Ellul, has said that we are living in a time when thought and action are being separated.[5] What we think is not necessarily what we do, and what we do often has no bearing on what we think. Os Guinness, a British evangelical sociologist living in the United States, echoes Ellul in suggesting that the link between knowing and doing is now broken. Guinness writes, "We are living in an age which knows more than ever before, yet less is done about what is known than ever before."[6]

On the one hand, we desperately need to heed the words of Guinness. It is time to do something with what we already know. Here is the call to action. Armchair radicals, put down your books, go to the coal face, and join the struggle! From you, let there be action from your reflection. Work at reducing the rhetoric-reality gap that seems to sum up many of your lives. Guinness writes that the Hebrew word for "to know" is also the word for caring:

> In the Hebrew understanding, to know something is to have power over it, and to have power over it is to have responsibility for it. Thus to know something is to care for it. The responsibility of knowledge can be found in specific teaching about knowing and doing. For example, in the book of James, "The man who knows the good he ought to do, but does not do it, is a sinner." For what we do with what we know is what Christian knowing is all about.[7]

On the other hand, however, let the activistic practitioner also be challenged. If the call for the armchair radical is to turn to the coal face, then the challenge for many a practitioner is to return to the library. It is time for the practitioner to not only love the Lord on the streets, but also love the Lord with their minds in the study. The private reflecting and reading of books and the communal sharing of ideas and experiences that can radicalize, energize and make a person's involvement more effective in public places.

The apostle Paul urges us to be adult in our thinking (1 Corinthians 14:20). But the last thing many of us in mission want to do is think. Because of this inability to critically reflect on the issues much of our mission is currently facing a crisis of effectivity. Our ranks are full of well-intentioned people who are largely ineffective. Much of what we do is either rendered a mess or irrelevant. In the words of Ignatius Loyola, the founder of the Jesuits, it is time to become "contemplatives in action." That is, we must be those who seek to understand their context and mission as they attempt to change their context by their mission.

This is not a call for all of us to drop our spades at the coal face and head for the nearest academic institution. As the New Testament theologian, Tom Wright, writes:

> The kingdom of God is not necessarily substantially advanced because another bright young Christian graduate completes her Ph.D. thesis, nor because some enterprising young lecturer publishes a learned article setting out his new interpretation of 2 Timothy 4.3.[8] [Rather, Wright urges us to see that] the challenge to think clearly is part of the calling to be Christian. The challenge to think Christianly is part of the calling to the church to take on the world with a gospel that makes sense; which makes sense of things for which the world of paganism has no answer. God has been renewing his church in its thinking, so that it can address the world the more clearly.[9]

NOTES

1 The Oxford Centre for Mission Studies is a project of the International Fellowship of Evangelical Mission Theologians. It provides a unique resource for the facilitation of Two-Thirds World church leaders and the ongoing interaction between First and Two-Thirds World agencies. The Centre is an affiliate of the United Kingdom Council for National Academic Awards and enables people to do post-graduate research degrees in their own context. The course of Theology and Development Studies is a two-year course for practitioners of development involving nine months in residence in Oxford and a further year of reflection in the context of the participant's ministry.

2 Christopher J. H. Wright, "The Use of the Bible in Social Ethics: Paradigms, Types and Eschatology," *Transformation* (Vol. 1, No. 1, 1984), p. 11.

3 Ibid., p. 77.

4 David Cook, *The Moral Maze: A Way of Exploring Christian Ethics* (London: SPCK, 1984), p. 85.

5 Jacques Ellul, *Propaganda: The Formation of Men's Attitudes* (Vintage Books, 1973), p. 27.

6 Os Guinness, "Knowing Means Doing," *On Being Guide to Training for Service* (Vol. 20, No. 7, August 1993), p. 6.

7 Ibid., pp. 6-10.

8 Tom Wright, *New Tasks for a Renewed Church* (London: Hodder & Stoughton, 1992), p. 115.

9 Ibid., p. 116.

Discipleship in Difficult Places

From the slums of Manila to the palaces and privileges of Oxford—was it really heaven? Not quite! Toward the end of our time in Oxford I was awakened one night by my wife's crying. Her honesty in expressing a desire not to return to the slums of Manila forced me to also voice my misgivings. We wanted to be with the poor and minister to them, but living in a slum seemed too much, especially because we knew what awaited us there.

Slums are an offense to God. They are abnormal and should not exist. For many they are places of death. Scripture rightly describes poverty as evil. Poverty is no virtue and no one can consider living in a slum to be the ultimate will of God for anyone, be they the poor or the missionary.

A radical spirituality

As we shared our misgivings with each other a taped sermon arrived from our church in New Zealand. In it, Murray Robertson made reference to Ezekiel 3:12-15. In this passage we read of Ezekiel having a wonderful worship experience with God. Then Ezekiel is led from this mountaintop into the valley of service. We are told that he went "in bitterness and in the anger of [his] spirit, with the strong hand of the Lord upon [him]." Suddenly we found ourselves in good company. It may be right to go to difficult places of discipleship but that does not necessarily mean that we want to go—even though God wills it.

We sensed God asking us to return to the slums, even though we did not want to. Some of our Christian friends found this position incomprehensible. I suspect it challenged the popular notion that people can reduce the will of God to whatever they want to do. Such a reduction is a subversion of the call of Christ. Some were under the impression that we had gone to the slums and stayed there because that is what we really wanted to do, just as they wanted to settle in their respective comfortable Western cities. They found it threatening that we also preferred their cities to the slums but still felt called to be with the poor of Asia because of certain aspects of our faith.

One of these aspects was worship. It has been said that you become what you worship. As we worship the Father we become as he is, in the sense of loving what he loves. The more we worship the more we love the world as he loves the world (John 3:16), and the more we love justice as he loves justice (Isaiah 61:8). Worship compelled us to return to the slums.

Another Old Testament servant inspired us. Nehemiah prayed for Jerusalem, and soon found himself on the road to Jerusalem. His private prayer life drove him to the public places. Spirituality leads to involvement.

A radical family living

When our son Joseph died, we feared it would encourage those who criticized our wisdom in taking our family to the slums of Manila. Many of those were fellow Christians.

Ruby and I stood firm. Families do not come first. We loved each other and the children, but we were not going to sacrifice some of our responsibilities as Christians on the altar of an unhealthy family concern.

Both of us had come from broken homes and even though our respective parents taught us many good things, we did not want to repeat some of their mistakes. For this reason we cherished the scriptural directives that talked about cleaving or joining together as husband and wife (Matthew 19:3-6), loving one another (Ephesians 5:21-29) and providing for the immediate needs of our young family (1 Timothy 5:8). In a world where the family so easily breaks apart we committed ourselves to this scriptural mandate for the family. This kind of responsible family living has kept us together for over thirteen years. As two people active in ministry we had no intention of sacrificing our family in the name of ministry, but neither did we want to give excessive regard to the family.

According to the Scriptures, we are to seek first the kingdom and not the family (Matthew 6:33). The kingly rule of God dictates where and how we live, not the rule of the family. Jesus, at times, had total disregard for some of the most revered family customs of his day. On one such occasion, he forbade a would-be disciple to even bury his own father (Matthew 8:21-22). In Jesus' day a son was expected to bury his father within 24 hours. This story is not meant to portray Jesus as some unfeeling monster, but to make clear that his mission will at times take priority over even some of our most sacred family customs.

Jesus underlines this theme when he says that to be his disciple a person must hate their own spouse, children or life (Luke 14:26-7). To "hate" means to leave, renounce and abandon. Now this Scripture does not give us a way out of a difficult marriage or family life, nor does it counsel us to sacrifice our families in the name of ministry. Rather, Jesus calls us to an exclusive commitment to him. Our allegiance is to none else! Costly discipleship and cross-bearing relate to all areas of life, even our precious marriages and families.

But cross-bearing has never been easy. Jesus tells the story of the great banquet in Luke 14:16-20. Among those that rejected the invitation to the banquet were those who had recently married. Possibly they excused themselves to spend more time together. And possibly behind this excuse lay a prior allegiance to feelings of security and materialism.

Times have not changed for, as most leaders and pastors tell us, many active single workers involved in strategic ministries get married and are seen no more. These newlyweds usually excuse themselves by quoting the Old Testament injunction that when a soldier in the Israelite army got married he should return from the front lines and be with his wife for a year. But the soldier did not return in order to create a nest of security, peace and affluence. He returned so the couple could have a baby, and his wife would not be left barren if he died in war (Israel's population growth had to be ensured while the Israelites were being continually threatened as a nation).

The balance of Scripture

On the one hand, we are to commit ourselves to our spouses, love and submit to them and provide for our families. On the other hand, while we are doing this we must seek first God's kingdom, give priority to the mission of Jesus and be exclusively committed to him. But have we got this balance right today? We like the set of verses (Matthew 19:3-6, Ephesians 5:21-29, 1 Timothy 5:8) that talk of joining, loving and providing. But what of the second cluster of verses (Matthew 6:33, 8:21-22; Luke 14:16-20, 26-7)? If the first set talks of responsible family living, then the other set demands radical family living (see Figure 8.1 on page 77).

Have we separated the family from the impact of the hard sayings of Jesus? We talk about a man and woman

Figure 8.1: The pressures on the family

Responsible Family Living	Radical Family Living
Cleaving *(Matthew 19:3-6)*	Kingdom First *(Matthew 6:33)*
Loving Family *(Ephesians 5:21-29)*	Hating Family *(Luke 14:26-27)*
Providing *(1 Timothy 5:8)*	Mission First *(Matthew 8:21-22)*

cleaving together, but they must also join a radical ministry. We talk about a man and woman loving and submitting to one another, but they must also submit to the Lord's radical demands for their lives. We talk about a couple providing for their family, but this same couple must also provide for the poor and needy in this world. Families are not to fall in love with themselves–they are to fall in love with Jesus. A family will know that it is loving Jesus when it loves the things Jesus loves: the world and justice.

We have no problem believing that practicing the first set of verses–those that touch on love, mutual submission and provision for the family–will protect our families. But we need to see that living out the second cluster of verses–those that touch on seeking God's will, prioritizing mission and giving allegiance to Jesus–will also protect the family.

You ask how? When we look at the lack of care in many non-Christian families we rightly conclude that this lack of care creates dysfunctional families. But an over-indulgence in care and protection by the Christian parent

can also create a dysfunctional Christian family. I wonder
if this is already beginning to happen. Are Christian parents creating a generation of weaklings by not exposing
their children to the poor and needy of this world? Have
we a generation of children that can only think in terms
of their needs and not the needs of others?

The Scripture verses that call Christian families to
costly and radical discipleship will keep these families
from seeing themselves as the center of the earth. Radical
family discipleship helps to keep need in its proper place.
Costly family discipleship will keep the family from over-
indulging in care and protection. In other words, mission
will place demands on the family that will save the family from itself.

A modern day Christian idol?

Idols are not just made out of wood and stone. An idol
is anything that so captures our allegiance that we begin
to compromise our Lord's commands. How does something become an idol? First, we give it an excessive
regard. Second, it becomes autonomous. We separate it
from the hard sayings of Jesus. Finally, it is idolatrous in
that it, and not the mission of Jesus Christ, now determines our behavior.

You often hear it said that "ministry is out of the question because of our family." Sometimes this kind of
response is valid but one wonders if many couples are
sacrificing some of our Lord's more costly commands on
the altar of an excessive regard for the family. Is the modern Christian family now a rival to the gospel and mission
of Jesus Christ? If so then it is also an idol. As Christians,
we often allow the good things of life to become our idols
and rivals to the mission of Jesus Christ.

Have we so reacted to stories of ministries that tragically sacrificed the family in the name of ministry that we

have now redefined the family and its needs in a way that holds us back from genuine radical discipleship? If so, then we must return to God's holistic view of the family where the members love and care for each other, yet at some cost also love the poor and needy in this world.

The Mother Teresa syndrome

Viv Grigg, the prophetic founder of Servants, wondered whether families with young children would survive in the slums. Colin Harrington, then international leader of Servants, thought it was worth the risk and invited us to come. Now Colin was urging our return. If someone had asked Mary (of Damayan Lagi), she would possibly have said we were mad to contemplate a return to her slum. Everything she wanted for her own family we were about to leave behind for the second time. She knew we had the money to live elsewhere and live better. She could not fathom why we would choose to live in a slum.

She was not alone. Our parents in New Zealand were also struggling with what we were doing. Before leaving for the Philippines, my Father visited us and gently requested that we listen to him. "Living in a Third World slum," he began, "is your choice, but your children have no choice. They have to go where you go. Therefore, is it right for you to take them to a place where they might suffer, and suffer through no fault or decision of their own?"

I was tempted to counter that it was unfair of him to compare all that was "good" in New Zealand with all that was supposedly "bad" in the Third World. Dad only had to read the newspapers to see that danger has no respect for location. Danger was not just "over there" but very much on the streets of New Zealand. I could have also said that God was not just calling Ruby and myself, but

the whole family, including our children. Instead, I
thanked him for his very real concern.

My mother, on the other hand, swung between placing
us alongside Mother Teresa and thinking that we were
somewhat strange (as some do of Mother Teresa). We dis-
agreed with being likened to the saintly woman, but
agreed that it was strange to go and live in a slum.

Ruby and I could understand why some of our immediate family were concerned about our living in the Third
World, especially those that did not consider themselves
as disciples of Jesus in the way we did. We did get upset
when we were questioned by some of our fellow believers
who asked whether we were putting our ministry ambi-
tions before our children. Jurgen Moltmann, a German
theologian, explains what was probably happening here:

> The "religion of the cross" scandalises; and most of
> all it scandalises one's "co-religionists" in one's own
> circle. But by this scandal, it brings liberation into a
> world which is not free. There is nothing so unpop-
> ular as for the crucified God to be made a present
> reality through faith.[1]

If it was a scandal for us to live in a slum, we only did
so because we wanted the other scandal to be wiped
clean from the face of the world: the scandal of poor families like Mary's, living as they do.

Who will take their place?

I had read of twelve couples who left the shores of
England in the nineteenth century to become missionaries in Africa. After eighteen months the tragic news
arrived in Britain. Ten of the twelve couples had died.
The Christian Missionary Society, the organization that
sent them out, had a crisis on their hands. Would the ministry in Africa survive?

To their amazement, people began to line up to take the place of those who had fallen. These people knew the facts and the figures. But like the twelve couples who had originally left, they had glimpsed the cross and were willing to die for the one who had died for them. Their commitment to the cross was echoed by another missionary, who argued: "If Christ be God and died for me, then no sacrifice can be too great for me to make for Him!"

I also read of Judson of Burma, who lost two wives and several children as he preached the gospel; Hudson Taylor, who lost his wife in China; Archbishop Oscar Romero, who was brutally killed in San Salvador as he spoke against injustice. Since 1987 in the Philippines, over forty Christian lay workers have lost their lives at the hands of Muslims.

Were all of these folk so wrong and are we so right? Were they so irresponsible and are we so responsible?

I read of a couple in the Philippines, the Ocampos. As Marxist leaders who were often on the run, they had only spent 22 months together in their entire twenty-plus years of marriage. And those 22 months together were spent in prison. I am not advocating such an extreme kind of sacrificial living. But there are many non-Christians living sacrificial lifestyles for the sake of their cause, yet it is we who claim to follow a crucified God.

If the gospel cost Jesus his life, then that gospel will also cost us dearly. It is time to stop playing safe religious games in our churches. It is time to stop using the rhetoric and begin to face reality. It is time to become a missionary church and not just settle for being a happy church. It is time to become a church of the cross and not just of our culture. It is time for all of us to join the struggle and take the place of those who have gone before us. We should do this because of the cross of Christ. If we claim the crucified Jesus as our Lord, then we must seek out the world's pain, take that pain into ourselves and give it over to Jesus, so that the world may be healed.

A radical finish

The final reason for our needing to return to Manila was that we felt a moral responsibility to finish what we had started. The apostle Paul got to the end of his life and could say: "I have finished the race." We wanted to echo that, but for us the story had just begun.

As I travel around and speak in various places I invariably see the same thing: unfinished stories scattered on church floors. People who started something, at much cost to themselves, having quit for various reasons. Our reading of Scripture showed a God who is not a quitter. So how could we not do the same? We booked our tickets, packed our bags, and said a teary goodbye to Oxford.

NOTES

1   Jürgen Moltmann, *The Crucified God* (London: SCM, 1974), p. 39.

Rejoining the Struggle

Upon arriving in Manila we went and spoke with Mary and Noel Cano, leading community activists in Damayan Lagi. "It's getting very serious!" was their first response to our questions. "Cory Aquino, it seems, has changed the laws that allow foreigners to buy our land."[1] They told us that the new Taiwanese owner now wanted everyone off the land. They advised us not to return to Damayan Lagi.

We decided to move back, but into a different neighborhood and a better house. Our eldest daughter, Emily, was now nine, and needed more space. We would continue to live a just and simple lifestyle, but one that we hoped would not cause resentment in our children. We managed to find a house that met our needs. So radical family living was changing to encompass responsible family living. However, we were still living in a Third World slum.

What did the future hold?

For Mary the future was more straightforward. Either she would have a home to live in or she would not. It was 1990 and all was not well for Mary and her slum. Her son startled her one day when he arrived with the amazing news that he had become a "born again" Christian and now had eternal life.

Mary had heard that these conversions were happening all over Manila, but she remained skeptical. Her son talked of some distant eternal future, but in the closing years of her life Mary could only recall the misery of the past. And now she was facing another life-and-death battle. There was talk of demolition and eviction from her slum. At her age she could not afford to be homeless. The hardships would kill her within a year.

Turning to her son she asked, "You think your Jesus has saved you, but can he also save our land?" Christians, she muttered away to herself, always talk about life after death, but what about a life before death? A life that now needed the land that was being threatened by demolition.

Disaster first became likely in 1988 when a Taiwanese company bought the land of Damayan Lagi. This was made possible by President Aquino's withdrawal of squatter protection to encourage foreign investment. The new owner wanted the fifteen hundred squatter families off the land so they could build 100 or so plush townhouses for the rich. At first no one took the threat seriously. But it quickly became a different matter. Definite moves were planned to evict the squatters of Damayan Lagi.

Fear began to stalk the streets of the slum. Imminent demolition spelled danger. One of Mary's boarders recalled the time she and her family had been evicted from Tatalon (the first slum that Servants worked in). Armed men arrived late at night to evict them. The men of the slum were grabbed and held in a holding pen. With them out of the way, the demolition crew proceeded to tear the roofs off the houses. Women and children screamed and fled. They had no time to save their few possessions. In the madness, a number of people were killed. The squatters were finally herded into a truck and dumped in a relocation site one hour's drive from Tatalon. With next to nothing, they had to start all over again.

Mary, however, feared the fires. It was common knowledge that some impatient land owners had torched the slums in the darkness of night. After people fled the fires, barricades would be put up to stop anyone from returning to rebuild. Fearing such an event, the men in Mary's neighborhood organized themselves into night watchmen and a fire prevention band. With the help of Servants they bought drums, fire extinguishers and fire pumps.

A deadly silence descended upon the slum. It was as if someone was in their death throes and everyone else was in mourning. People were paralyzed by fear of the unknown. But some refused to believe that demolition was imminent. In their denial, they continued to live as though nothing had happened. As if to signal this they built extra rooms onto their houses or placed concrete on a muddy pathway.

The more astute leaders of the community treated the threat of demolition very seriously. They had to fight the problem, but first they had to agree on a strategy.

Mary, like many others in Damayan Lagi, owned her house even though she did not own the land it was built on. She was squatting on this land. Because she had lived on this land for nearly forty years, Mary did not see herself as a squatter. Rather, she was a long-term tenant and homeowner. She argued that if the man from Taiwan wanted her off the land, then he would have to provide her and the other homeowners with a new place to live. All the homeowners united around this demand. They formed themselves into an alliance to press their case.

"But what of the others?" Mary was asked. "The renters and sharers, for example, those who do not own a house. What do you expect the new owner to do for them?"

"Well, I know it's hard, but that is not our concern," retorted Mary. "The homeowners are the priority here."

Mary believed that those who had something and were about to lose it should be given something in return. But why should those who have nothing, like the renters, be given something?

Noel Cano saw it differently. To him, Mary and those like her had internalized the very values of their oppressors. Just as the owner was out for profit at the expense of others, so Mary was now putting her own welfare before that of others who were poorer and more powerless than she was.

Noel, an experienced community organizer, knew that if they were to successfully fight the owner then both homeowner and renter would have to unite. A divided slum would only play into the hands of the aggressor. He proposed a coalition representing all sectors within Damayan Lagi, both homeowners and renters.

Unfortunately, many of the homeowners, including Mary, did not trust Noel. So began a battle for the hearts and minds of slum dwellers. Both the homeowners' alliance and Noel's coalition canvassed Damayan Lagi for recruits and support.

On the sidelines the owner backed the alliance against the coalition. They could only smile—their tactics of divide and conquer were proving effective. Giving land to just the homeowners was financially more prudent for them than giving land to all.

The coalition grew. Furthermore, Noel, an astute politician, went to both the mayor's office and the national government and received their official recognition of his coalition. The coalition was now a force to be reckoned with. The owner could no longer ignore them.

"It's up to the people," the Taiwanese lawyers finally said to both the alliance and the coalition. "Let the people elect a representative. If the homeowners win, then we will negotiate with them; otherwise, we'll talk to the coalition."

All parties agreed to an election the following Wednesday.

Either way, it finally dawned on the people that eviction and demolition were inevitable. It was now only a matter of when it would happen. No matter who won the election, Damayan Lagi would be flattened.

Political missionaries

Since 1986, the Servants workers in Damayan Lagi had engaged in a number of activities: preaching the Good News about Jesus, doing good deeds, stimulating income generation projects and many other projects. Our presence and projects had had an impact on the community. Never before had Westerners actually come to live in their slum. But now, because of the land issue, something new was being asked of us.

Both the alliance and the coalition requested that we join them. What were we to do? At first it seemed more Christian to be neutral and not take sides. But the stakes were high. People were about to lose everything–their land, security, jobs and schooling. The bulldozers would not only dismantle their memories in Damayan Lagi but also dash their hopes for the future. Sitting on the fence seemed a cowardly response.

"What do we do?" I asked Noel.

"You must take a position!" he said.

We had come to Manila believing that we should concentrate on the greatest need, to side with the victims of other people's sins, to be in relational and compassionate solidarity with the poorest of the poor. In light of this, we had no choice but to side with the renters and Noel's coalition. This did not mean that we no longer cared for Mary and the alliance. Rather, the priority at this moment was to be in solidarity with those who had the least. We were called to take affirmative action on behalf of those most adversely affected by the threat of demolition. This positive discrimination was needed if we were to help the most vulnerable.[2]

Everyone waited. Would the owner really respect the result of the election and negotiate anew, or would he get his hired thugs to torch the slum? Who would win the election?

A new set of questions

The day before the election we met some missionaries from another organization and told them of our situation. Their response was similar to what we had encountered from fellow missionaries and some Filipino national pastors. "What can you expect if you're doing something illegal?" they responded. "You're even breaking the law yourselves by squatting on the land. And not only that, you're encouraging others to continue to do so."

Their questions, of course, raised some significant issues. In the name of relational solidarity with the poor, was it right to break the law as Christians and squat on someone else's land? In adopting an incarnational model of mission had we ceased being law-abiding citizens and become Christian criminals?

Technically we were operating outside the law. But we felt we were doing this in a country where the law was not working. Why should squatters cooperate with a legal system that often ignores its own laws, protects the elite and must often be bribed to get anything done? Are squatters really breaking the law when a moral legal code does not exist? And have squatters any choice in a land that has laws to ensure property protection for the elite but lacks laws of land provision for the poor? Technically, therefore, we were breaking the law, but in a context of social injustice. We hoped that in some small way, our relational solidarity with squatters would draw attention to this injustice.

The day came for the election. Tony, the pastor of the fellowship that Servants had helped bring into being in Damayan Lagi, came with questions. Why would God lead us to a place, help us build a church, see more than eleven community cooperatives established, give us money to erect new housing, schools and multi-purpose buildings, establish income generating projects, bring in legal water and power–and then allow it all to be brutally dismantled?

Holding back the tears, we too confessed to the same questions. Six years of hard work were now scheduled for destruction. Despite all that would remain in people's lives, much would be lost. It was all very depressing. In some small way we were beginning to feel what it was like to be at the mercy of poverty. Our work with the poor over the past six years was now to become yet another victim of poverty. Like the poor, we would lose the past but, unlike many of the poor, we still had a future.

As for Tony's question about how God could have led us to Damayan Lagi only to see all our work dismantled, we asked why should we expect God to lead us to safe and profitable places and not do the same for the poor? Was it right for us to expect preferential treatment from God and not expect the same for millions of poor people?

Tony wasn't the only one asking questions. After sharing with our own Servants team about what was happening in Damayan Lagi, one of our missionary colleagues asked whether we had made the right decision in going back to Damayan Lagi on our return from Oxford.

In returning we knew that there was a threat of demolition hanging over the place. But as we had spent just under three years in Damayan Lagi before going to Oxford, we felt we had a moral responsibility to finish the journey we had started with the poor. Jesus had said that the poor would always be with us; for us, that was reason enough to be always with them.

We knew that the bulldozers would probably destroy anything we created, and that at the end of our journey in Damayan Lagi we would not have a movement or monument to show for our many efforts. These thoughts hurt.

An early disappointment

On our first Sunday after returning to Damayan Lagi we attended the small Christian fellowship that we had helped to establish some years before. We were especially interested to see how far they had come with the experimentation in learning and education that had been set in motion before our departure for Oxford.

This experiment involved everyone sitting in a circle and facing each other. Before this our gatherings had resembled a bus ride. Everyone sat behind each other in rows while the pastor took us where he wanted us to go. Our first time in a circle was memorable. Embarrassment and a sense of awkwardness filled the room. It was much easier seated in rows, one behind another–that way you could hide. All the activity was at the front and all you had to do was respond dutifully when called on to do so.

Sitting in a circle was different. Two hours into our time, however, there was a buzz in the air. During the meeting we had simply asked a question, and illustrated it with a picture. The group was then asked to reflect on the question and attempt to formulate a response. Initially silence reigned, but one by one everyone grappled with the problem until we had a full-blown debate on our hands. Two hours later people were still arguing as they left the room. We had never seen this before. The following Sunday we asked why they had become so excited over the circle experiment.

Figure 9.1: Formal versus. informal gathering

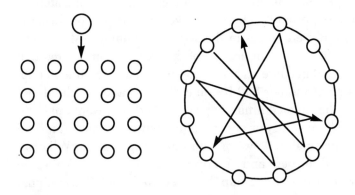

Formal Gathering
one leader, many listeners

Informal Gathering
many speakers, many listeners

Formal Gathering	Informal Gathering
Passive	Active
Secure	Threatening
Monologue	Dialogue
Top-down	Bottom-up
Authoritarian	Communitarian
Voicelessness	Voice
Respect for the preacher	Respect for one another
Beneficiaries	Givers
Learners	Teachers
Disempowering	Empowering

"I heard my own voice," came the amazing reply of one young woman. "Up until now," she continued, "I've had to listen to other voices. No one wanted to listen to my voice, the voice of a poor person. But last Sunday I was listened to."

A small step is a huge human gain among the poor. In this one small act of making a circle we had facilitated a dynamic whereby the poor were speaking to one another, listening to one another, learning from one another and respecting one another. Each face had communicated: "I am important!" These discovered voices soon became empowered voices in the wider community. After a few months, for example, one of the women commented that she had become an active member of a community cooperative, another had become active in a local school and another in a community project. And so it went on.

These were our encouraging memories as we returned to the small fellowship with much expectation. What we saw disturbed and disappointed us deeply. While we were away the group had reverted to the traditional approach of the pastor doing everything from the front. Two hours later we left very much aware that the group had not owned the changes we had implemented before our departure for Oxford.

I feared that our departure had severely disrupted the whole transition from the traditional approach to the "face to face" model. Perhaps we should have stayed with the people to help them through the transition phase. It seemed our departure had created a climate of insecurity and, understandably, they had returned to the familiar and secure traditional approach. Unfortunately, our need for empowering study at Oxford had unintentionally disempowered the poor in their journey of change.

"Where to from here?" we wondered. We decided to remain at the edge of the group and attend occasionally.

Interestingly, as the months went by the people slowly returned to the more interactive face to face approach without our intervention. Dialogue, small groups, listening, creativity and brainstorming featured more and more in their gatherings.

"Why the change?" we asked.

"Before you went to Oxford you helped us see problems with the traditional approach," they told us. "But we still hadn't seen it for ourselves. When you left you gave us the space to make our own mistakes, to learn from them and thus see the need for change."

For change to occur and be long-term it must be personal and corporate. People must agree together that they need change. Need-based change is preferable to advice-driven change.

From the bottom up

Since returning to Damayan Lagi we had wanted to see some success with our projects. It is good to have a theology of failure, but success is also good. At the top of our agenda was to capitalize on what we had learned since our early mistakes. Noel Cano, our community organizer in Damayan Lagi, provided a way for this to happen.

"We want to form a cooperative so we can obtain legal electricity," he informed me.

I was impressed. "So where do we come in?"

"We can come up with half the funds necessary," Noel said proudly, "but we are hoping that you can provide the rest."

Since returning to Manila we had already successfully undertaken some community projects in Sapang Palay.[3] These included concrete paving, basketball courts and bridges. All of these projects followed a standard process, using a set of basic, but important, guidelines.

1 The entire community must meet to agree on the project.
2 The community should elect its own management committee.
3 The community must be willing to make some financial contribution to the project, with the amount to be agreed on in negotiation with Servants.

4 The community must have prepared a maintenance
  plan for the time following the completion of the
  project. This was to ensure that the project would
  not deteriorate and become just another failed
  endeavor.

An unwillingness to follow these basic guidelines
would result in the withdrawal of the Servants organization. We felt that these practical guidelines reflected the
principles we had learned.

As Noel read the process guidelines, he smiled. He had
also been trying to implement projects in tune with these
guidelines. We were in agreement.

In six months we created about eleven community
cooperatives. Most of these were formed around the need
for legal electricity or water. All were started and managed by the people themselves. Altogether, the poor had
given more than two hundred thousand pesos (approximately US$40,000) to make these cooperatives possible.
This was the "bottom up" approach that we had learned
from our errors.

But two other results truly delighted us. First, not one
person from these cooperatives became a member of our
local church fellowship. What—this is success? Yes, at
last! Of course we wanted people to become Christians
and attend church, but through genuine repentance and
faith, not because of our project assistance. Our project
process was finally putting an end to the rice Christian
syndrome.

The second delight was that these cooperatives were
bringing about a shift in local politics. People were now
depending on themselves and their own initiative. Consequently, the traditional and corrupt local government
lost much of its influence. People participation was rub-
bing out local corruption.

This did not happen easily. The cooperative on Eleventh Street, under the leadership of Mary's son, Charlie, had eighty members. Each member had contributed eight hundred pesos. In a few months they would receive legal power. However, Charlie's brother-in-law, Pedro, wanted it all stopped. His livelihood depended on his share of the collective bribe for illegal power. Legal electricity would rob him of income. He would have to get a job. He remembered how he had stopped this project last time at gunpoint, and decided to repeat the process.

Grabbing his revolver Pedro headed toward Charlie's house, intending to force him to back down. Charlie made clear his determination to withstand Pedro's attack, causing Pedro to back down. He threatened to return but

Concrete paving: one of the neighborhood cooperatives

A fire prevention pump: another cooperative project

never did. Another shift in local politics took place—
Pedro lost his influence and Charlie became the new
community leader.

The first power bill arrived and the members noted
with alarm how much everyone had to pay. Illegal power
was so much cheaper. But they had expected this. Asked
why they preferred the more expensive legal power, they
replied that it was not only safer and more reliable but
also decent. They were illegal squatters, branded as criminals. But now, at least in the matter of electricity, they
were doing things right. It felt good.

Today, only one of these cooperatives has failed. They
have become an integral part of the community, and an
important part of the slum's political power base. The
cooperatives were run by the people and increasingly
financed by them.

We had only had a small part in the establishment of these cooperatives. Initially, we simply joined the community life by being with the people and walking the streets. As we walked we became listeners. In time we got to know key people who could emerge as potential community organizers. We moved alongside these folk and talked the talk of community development. Then we stepped back to allow the community organizers to work with their neighborhoods on their first community project. After that, we became increasingly secondary. As soon as we had our first group of community cooperatives running, the people became responsible to repeat the process with others. For example, when Mary's son, Charlie, got his cooperative up and running we asked him to advise another area in Damayan Lagi on how they could establish one.

As the people helped each other, Ruby and I were reduced to being just bankers; to reading project proposals; ensuring the guidelines were followed; and, if all was fine, to giving money. While we knew this would be the logical conclusion of community development we were left wondering what we were doing in the slums. Before this revolution of the heart we had been so active, vocal and, it seemed, needed. Now we were secondary, temporary, merely advisors and, of course, bankers.

Some may wonder how this banker role differs from the previous role of dispensers of charity. Before, we had been the givers and the poor the receivers. Now they were still receivers but they were also givers, decision makers, managers of a process, implementers and owners of the cooperatives. Above all, they had learned to initiate action.

When we now talk about community development in conferences in the West, people get excited. They want to jump on the bandwagon and get involved. But in the

back of their minds they still have the idea that *they* will
do community development for the poor. That is a contradiction in terms. We do not do community development for the poor. If we think we do, then this type of
development becomes, yet again, a top-down paternalis-
tic affair. Community development, rightly understood, is
exactly that—*community* development. It is something
done by the community for the community. If outsiders
have any role in it, it will always be a small one.

Now we were really becoming servants. A servant not
only gives up what he or she has, but also renounces who
he or she is. Comparatively speaking, it is easier to give
money or even time to someone, but it is very different to
give up who one is as a person. It is not easy to give up
being a key player, a full-time active participant, a teacher
or a leader, for the sake of a development process. But if
the poor are to increase in stature, then we must decrease.
Their empowerment may demand that we lay aside who
we are. This denying of self, refusing to use what one has
or be who one is, is the mark of a genuine community
developer. The call is to be a person who moves away
from the center of focus and out to the edge.

The election

Our enthusiasm over the cooperatives was always
tempered by the uncertainty over the land issue. We
hoped the election would settle things. There was antici-
pation in the air, the crowds were gathering, the platform
was set. Each faction still engaged in feverish last-minute
preparations for the big night. Senators, congressmen and
local government officials all turned up. Much was at
stake in this election. Whatever faction won would not
only negotiate with the owners but would also become a
key influence in the community for the upcoming
national elections.

After wishing Noel Cano good luck, I sat down and readied myself for a long night. It was going to be a close fight. Noel, the leader of the coalition that wanted land for all, including the poorest of the poor, sat pensively smoking one cigarette after another. The alliance, who wanted land only for the homeowners, sat together and were just as nervous. Mary was among them.

The owner's lawyers began to count the votes: "Cano, 250; the alliance, 245." An hour later it was still anyone's contest: Cano, 500; the alliance, 492. And then finally, one hour later, the winner was declared: "Cano, 875; the alliance, 840." We had won! It was a close call, yes, but still a victory.

Noel attributed the victory to the formation of the community cooperatives: "If it wasn't for their joining forces into a political bloc, we would not have won." In his speech before the vote count, Noel even made mention of Servants: "If it wasn't for Servants, the cooperatives may not have come into existence." I wanted to stand up and take issue with that. In my mind, the cooperatives would not be in existence if not for the people. But Noel was just being polite by thanking us publicly.

God's footprints in the world

As I left the basketball court I was tempted to praise God for the election result. I say tempted because I was not too sure whether this victory was from God or not. It is one thing to say that human history is the arena of God's activity, but quite another to identify, as David Bosch puts it, God's footprints in the world. I had read of how some Catholic priests had called the Nicaraguan revolution "a sign of God's providential intervention in history." But this sign has since been discredited. Similarly, many Filipinos had called the Edza revolution "a divine affair." Few today, however, would describe it that way.

Was the power of the people in Damayan Lagi the power of God? David Bosch suggests the following sign-posts for identifying God's activity: "Where people are experiencing and working for justice, freedom, community, reconciliation, unity, and truth, in a spirit of love and selflessness, we may dare to see God at work."[4] The coalition, under Noel's leadership, wanted justice for all and to work with the alliance in a spirit of selflessness. As a nominal Christian, Noel had given up his job to work voluntarily on behalf of the poor in Damayan Lagi. So, yes, I gave in to the temptation to thank God for the election victory, but did so in a provisional and tentative sort of way.

The second round

Winning the election proved to be the easy part. That contest was against a local politician. Now we had to fight the owner, not on the streets of Damayan Lagi but around a negotiation table in his office. Our voices would not be heard, only the voices of lawyers–theirs and ours.

After months of discussion the owner agreed not only to give two hectares[5] to the poor, but also to sell two and a half hectares to the residents of Damayan Lagi. Noel believed that the total of four and a half hectares could house most of the poor. Our celebrations, however, were cut short when we were told the price of the two and a half hectares for sale: the owner wanted fifty million pesos (US$1,900,000)! There was no way that the 2,000 families in Damayan Lagi could come up with that amount, especially since more than 50 percent of the people were unemployed or not fully employed. Those that did have a job received no more than 2,500 pesos a month, and even that was not enough to live on. The owner knew we could never afford that price.

When we told the owner that we could not buy the land, he responded with what seemed a very generous counteroffer. "I am willing to donate three and a half hectares," he declared. We could not believe it. This was a victory! It was not the four and a half hectares we had been fighting for, but it was a good compromise. Three and a half acres could still house most of the poor. But there was a catch.

"Mr. Cruz must be willing to join the coalition," said the owner's lawyers. Noel Cano and the coalition withdrew to ponder the situation. They knew Mr. Cruz.

After the election, Mr. Cruz made it known that he did not respect Noel's victory. He formed his own faction and began to fight the owner in the courts. This served only to anger the owner and frustrate Noel in his negotiations. But it soon became clear what lay behind Cruz's tactics. He had been negotiating a different deal with his political contacts in the mayor's office. Instead of dividing the three and a half hectares equally and distributing to all, Cruz wanted the land to be divided in proportion to the current land ownership. If a poor family only had twenty square feet now, then that should be what they get on the new land. No one had to look far to see Cruz's motivation. His current landholding was one of the biggest in Damayan Lagi.

Furthermore, Cruz did not want the land given directly to the people. We suspected he wanted the mayor's office to have responsibility for the redistribution. Cruz and the mayor had already had many mutually beneficial business dealings.

It was in the owner's interest to use Cruz's opposition to Noel. The owner knew Cruz would more than likely never agree to join Noel's coalition, so the people would never meet the conditions whereby they would receive the three and a half hectares. The owner's bargaining position would thus be much stronger and the people would ultimately have to back down and be content with what they were finally given.

Noel could not believe it. The poor wanted justice and fair play, but these hardly featured in other people's calculations. Cruz wanted more land for himself. The mayor, it seemed, wanted to control the distribution of the land because that would give him political power over Damayan Lagi. The owner wanted to control the negotiations. And all Noel and the poor wanted was security for the future and to be able to live somewhere.

NOTES

1 This is what we believed, but we found it difficult to document.

2 Richard Harries, *Is There a Gospel for the Rich?* (London: Mowbray, 1992), explores the tension between equality and this positive discrimination.

3 This is where we lived for the first nine months of our time in Manila in 1985. We had kept our links with the people in this area and worked with them on occasion.

4 Bosch, *Transforming Mission*, pp. 430-31

5 One hectare equals approximately 2.5 acres.

The Poor Cousins:
Mercy and Evangelism

Despite the imminent changes, community development was our priority. Some saw this as a replacement for mercy ministries and evangelism. Others argued that in the process of emphasizing development we were in danger of greatly reducing the significance of mercy and evangelism, making them poor cousins to the major effort. We needed to define community development.

While community development is not the solution to world poverty, neither is it in opposition to mercy ministries or evangelism or in isolation from other ministries. Community development is one way to enable the transformation of a people and their nation. It is only one part of our holistic mandate to empower the poor.

Furthermore, development principles are needed to guide other ministries. For example, a high view of people, group dynamics and a "bottom up" approach to learning and action are just as relevant to mercy giving as they are to community projects. Our mercy ministries must be developmental and our development must be merciful.

Revisiting mercy

Remember Mary's son-in-law with the drinking problem and the gun (see chapter 4)? We had fed his problem, not helped it. This is often the result when Christians choose the path of mercy with no conditions. Others struggle with constantly applying conditions to the mercy they pass out. In the slums, we have had to learn to reconcile these two positions. Both approaches agree that the goal of mercy is to empower the needy person.

Not long after the disastrous affair with Mary's son-in-law, we received yet another knock on our door. Standing before us was a young man, his wife and their three malnourished children. They had just arrived from the war-torn countryside and were in a desperate state. They had no relatives to turn to. They had heard of the soft-hearted white Westerners, swallowed their pride and came begging for help. What should we do? To be merciful meant asking hard questions. How could we best help them? How could they become independent of us and not dependent, empowered and not disempowered?

"Here is one hundred pesos for food tonight and tomorrow we will work out something together," we finally said.

The next day we visited the family. Their pathetic excuse for a room lay over an open sewer. Gaping holes marked their floor and all four walls were in disrepair and sloping in all directions. There was nothing inside the room—just the family and their poverty. Crumpled up in one dark corner lay their youngest, in a severe state of third degree malnutrition. What should we do?

We told some of the neighbors of the plight of these new arrivals. By the end of the week much had transpired. The neighbors took it upon themselves to help feed the family. One of the men got the man a job as a painter at his place of work. We asked Jo Ward, a doctor with Servants, to begin a monitored program of nutrition and feeding as the youngest was suffering from malnutrition.

In this instance community had become the mediating structure between overwhelming need and us. There was some financial aid, but also much more: communal sharing, job creation and intensive care. Because of this merciful start the family could eventually move on to a better area and house. Empowerment had taken place.

Mercy giving is as much about the right process of giving as about the project itself. Unfortunately, a lot of mercy giving is characterized by knee-jerk reactions to need. Instead of reflecting on a need we react to it and give impulsively. We were learning to give in a considered way so that people could move on from relief to a degree of self-sufficiency.

But when should we withdraw our giving? Many times we were tempted to stop because of ingratitude. In the eyes of some we, the rich, were obligated to help them.

Stopping for this reason was tantamount to revenge withdrawal and had no place in our Christian framework. Nor should we necessarily stop because we were feeling pain in giving. Much of the money given for mercy was coming from our own pockets. Deep in our hearts we knew that selfish withdrawal had no place in our framework either. Rather, as Timothy Keller counsels, "we may cut off aid if it is unmerciful to continue it".[1] In other words, mercy should limit mercy.

Emergency relief

One night there was a fire in the *dulo* (this is a separate area at the end of the street). Fires in slums were like lighting a match in a matchbox. One small fire soon consumes all it touches and is only possibly contained by the narrow street borders. This fire began with a gas bottle explosion and thankfully was not in our block.

We sighed with relief. This fire would not touch our house. Three hundred other families, though, lost everything they had. The disaster reduced many to being people of the ash heap—the poorest of the poor. Tragically, some of the houses could have been saved. We learned later that the fire engines only came when the wealthy family in the mansion across the road agreed to bribe the firemen.

Noel Cano, still the faithful community organizer, arrived on the scene and straight-away organized a barricade around the land that had been devastated by the fire. He feared that the owner would come and reclaim his land, which often happened when squatters lost their homes.

Next morning, we went to the devastated area. Everything had been flattened except for a few concrete block walls. Damp black ash clung to everything. Families huddled together in the midst of the smoldering heaps. Some people were digging into the ash with their bare hands in the hope of resurrecting something.

We discussed our plan of action. Some Christian groups would see this as an ideal opportunity for evange-

The aftermath of the fire

Rebuilding after the fire

lism. They could print a religious tract entitled, "You have had one fire—escape the next!" (meaning the eternal judgment one). But we have very little in common with this kind of religious response to disasters. Yet neither could we apply our community development principles of encouraging to self-reliance as the fire victims were desolate—they had nothing but themselves.

This seemed a legitimate case for mercy giving. We expressed our willingness to give over 100,000 pesos to help folk erect walls and roofs. It was still the rainy season and they need shelter urgently.

The people could give only themselves to the project. We encouraged them to organize the buying and distribution of materials, and the management of the project. They could take upon themselves the task of rebuilding, even though they could not contribute material resources.

Five days later, simple structures were springing up from the ash heap. Our contribution and their involvement sparked a spirit of hope among the people. They would rebuild their community. This kind of merciful partnership ensured that our financial giving did not disempower them. They brought themselves, their networks, skills, dedication and organization to the project. The success of the whole operation spoke more of their efforts than of our generosity.

Revisiting evangelism

Community development was proving to be time consuming. It was much easier and quicker to give money, medicines and clothes than to be involved by helping the poor come together to learn, discuss and act. Some began to wonder whether our focus on community development would inevitably take us away from the cause of verbally proclaiming Christ and making disciples. Maybe the old charge that social responsibility eventually becomes a distraction to evangelism would finally be our undoing.

I, too, was wondering whether this was occurring. From 1985 to 1993 we had not seen much effective evangelism come out of our community involvement. In the first phase, which was characterized by social relief projects, we saw the wrong type of conversion–the creation of rice Christians. Since our social action days with community development and cooperatives, there were very few conversions. We had hope that many of the lost and needy would receive a double blessing–a better life before death, and the promise of eternal life after death. We had seen some progress on the former, but very few had come to know Christ. Our team reacted in one of three ways to this disturbing situation:

1. Returning to "just evangelism"

Because of holism's apparent failure to deliver converts, some got disillusioned and were tempted to leave the community projects and return to our former salvation theology that asks only that people be saved.

2. Redefining evangelism

Evangelism, for some, was fast becoming merely value transformation. In other words, evangelizing the poor and needy now demanded the careful communication and transfer of Christian values to those who live in our communities. Some of these values included respect, community, forgiveness, self-determination and dignity.

They failed to see, however, that although these values are good in themselves, by themselves they are not enough to bring about the needed transformation. Discussing values with a prostitute, substance abuser or youth at risk is fruitless when they do not have the grace to own and grow those values in themselves. Increased awareness about values, without the power to develop and nurture them, creates a frustration that can easily turn to resentment. Jesus Christ provides that power.

3. Rejecting evangelism

We were seeing progress through a focus on social concern. Jobs had been created, new houses built, loans given, and people and communities empowered. We were tempted to settle for this and leave evangelism to those called and gifted to do it. Ironically, we had seen others start with "just evangelism," then marry that with social responsibility and end up in the "just social responsibility" camp. Extreme positions that argue for just this or that are a reductionism that disempower both the Christian worker and the poor and needy.

From the start some had been critical of Christians getting involved in community projects and social concern now reminded us of their claim that these would, at best, prove a distraction to evangelism and, at worst, end up betraying evangelism altogether. We felt that social concern was not a distraction or betrayal of evangelism. We believed that social concern takes us into the world of the non-Christian—into their issues, debates, networks, gathering places, felt needs and heart cries, and into their sin and dark corners.

Admittedly, this entry into their world can be a most reckless venture. We embark on this journey at the risk of being hijacked along the way by that which is alien to God. As the critics charge, we may even be diverted by an alien vision that focuses on social concern with little or no place for evangelism. This is a risk. But the answer is not to abandon the journey, but know how better to walk it. When things go wrong it is not a matter of dismissing community involvement, but of identifying the things that keep people from coming to Christ and rectifying those things.

NOTES

1 Timothy Keller, *Ministries of Mercy: The Call of the Jericho Road* (Grand Rapids: Zondervan, 1989), p. 98.

Where to from Here?

I do not believe that the solutions to the reactions and problems mentioned in the previous chapter lie in reexamining the theory of holism. I am assuming that most of us are already committed to a holistic mandate with a suitable biblical framework. That is, we believe people need deliverance from sin, demons and oppressive social structures. We believe, therefore, that mission must include both word and deed, the verbal and visual, proclamation and demonstration.

I am also assuming that most of us agree that evangelism and social responsibility are "equally important but genuinely distinct aspects of the total mission of the church."[1] Both are imperative and neither is primary. Finally, when it comes to social responsibility I am assuming that we do not think that "God is out to lunch." For us, social responsibility is just as "spiritual" as evangelism and in need of God's anointing, counsel and Spirit.

Some may argue that we are assuming far too much here. I don't think so. Over the years, I have been encouraged by all the good work in the area of holistic ministry. No longer do the one-dimensional churches, organizations and mission groups thrive. It is now rare for Christian groups to focus on just one aspect of mission. Instead, many of our mission groups are multi-dimensional and holistic in nature. In light of these assumptions, there is no need to rework our theory of holism.

Figure 11.1: Jesus and holism

Organi-zation	Deliverance From	Through	With	Motive	Type of Compassion
(1) Aid-Mercy	Material Hardship	Organization and Logistics	Money	Mercy	Comfortable Compassion
(2) Pentecostal	Demons	Celebration	Power	Compelled by Spirit	Charismatic Compassion
(3) Baptist Preaching	Sin	Salvation	Word	Command	Conversational Compassion
(4) Radical	Injustice	Demonstra-tion Protest	Deeds	Anger	Critical Compassion

NOTE: Jesus ministers holistically in John 5:1-18

(1) Verse 6: Jesus seeks to alleviate the man's immediate need.
   The aid and mercy people applaud this.
(2) Verses 8-9: Jesus heals the man.
   The Pentecostals shout "Amen!" and love this part.
(3) Verse 14: Jesus preaches to the man and calls for repentance.
   The Baptists commend this Jesus.
(4) Verse 16: Jesus heals on the Sabbath and thus comes into conflict
   with "The System."
   The radicals admire this Jesus.

We will not find solutions to the apparent betrayal of evangelism by going back over the theory. We are not setting out to redefine holism. That work has already been done.[2] Instead, more work needs to be done on the *practice* of holism. Today's challenge is not to know more about holism but to know what to do with what we already know.

Some answers

The following lays out some of the ways we sought to effectively engage in community projects so that men and women would come to Christ. It is not definitive, exhaustive or conclusive. We have only recently learned these lessons so they are in need of more testing.

To make the connection between evangelism and community projects more effective we needed to examine two equally important factors: first, the Christian worker(s) attempting to make this connection; and second, the models used to bring about this connection.

The workers

In the end, the Christian worker is more important than the program, model or method. Good projects and models by themselves do not make for effective evangelism—good workers do. Why is it, then, that many good people, community workers and neighborhood radicals do not make good evangelists? I suggest it may be because of the following.

1. A lack of time

Christians with heavy community involvement are busy people. They are busy with issues, causes and committees—so busy that invariably they do not have time for people. "And if you don't have time for people," writes Raymond Fung, "you can forget about evangelism."³ The solution appears to be to become less busy, but Fung argues that the answer may be more spiritual in nature than that. He urges the worker to recapture the principle of "disturbability" or availability.

In our early years of ministry we were only too glad for people to drop in and talk. We needed all the friends, language assistance and help we could get. This openness and willingness to be interrupted made for some dramatic early conversions. As the mission and development load grew, so our days became increasingly dictated to by the appointment book. It was also at this time that those amazing conversations with people began to dry up.

The Gospel writers tell of a Jesus whose life was a story of interruption. But out of interruption came a movement that changed the world. The small interruptions of life have an influence quite disproportionate to their size. This is the miracle of interruption!

2. A lack of confidence

If visitors detect in the worker a shyness or reluctance to talk about such words as "salvation" and "Jesus" then, as Fung writes, "they will understand and will not embarrass us with the subject."[4] We must remember that working with many of the poor and needy means dealing with a sensitive people who do not like to be shamed and therefore do not wish to shame others. If they sense that we are ill at ease when talking about our spirituality they will keep away from this subject to avoid embarrassing us.

After the "awful mistake" episode, I lost my confidence in God and his Word. I doubted my heritage and God's promises. The poor picked this up straight-away and from then my hesitancy set the agenda for our conversations.

The solution lies not in adding more "God talk" to our conversations, but rather in nurturing that passion within us to share our faith with others. I have observed that those Christians who keep alive the joy of their own salvation are the ones who will take every opportunity to tell others about their God of mercy, forgiveness and healing. All that God has done in Christ for them still overwhelms them, and so their only response is that of gratitude expressed in telling others about this good God.

We see this in the life of the apostle Paul. He could not fail to tell others that Jesus had given himself for Paul (Galatians 2:20), and that God's love had been poured into Paul's heart (Galatians 5:5). David Bosch writes, "He [Paul] has exchanged the terrible debt of sin for another debt, the debt of gratitude, which manifests itself in mission."[5] I recaptured this idea some two years after the "awful mistake" days.

The joy of Paul's salvation was still very much alive long after his conversion to Christ. When we lose that joy we also lose that sense of gratitude to God, which is a key motivational factor in evangelism. Furthermore, if we lose that joy and are rendered mute in our evangelism, we send out mixed signals. Then, writes Fung, "people outside the church are confused by these signals and do not know what to expect if they take the first hesitant step."[6]

3. A lack of identification

Community workers and neighborhood radicals are often very earnest and dedicated people, driven by passion and ideals. A purist streak runs through most of us. Although these characteristics are commendable and not necessarily damaging to others, they can be. Fung suggests that many radicals have "an absolutist, totalitarian or fundamentalist streak which does not make much sense to the average person."[7] Some people may feel inferior, inadequate or threatened by the radical, because the radical defines a relationship more by difference than sameness. This minimizes identification, and where there is little or no identification, Fung argues, there is no evangelism.

I feel that we radicals need to work extra hard at defining ourselves by how similar we are to others. This will demand getting in touch with our flawed humanity and seeing ourselves as no different from the rest of humankind. Unfortunately, many community workers and radicals find this extremely difficult to do, for we have a high view of ourselves but often tend to have, or convey, a low view of others.

We forget that we, too, are a mix of good and evil, that we are still full of unhealed, dysfunctional, twisted wills and sin. Yet while engaged with our community or neighborhood we see only the latter's dysfunction and not our own.

The community worker and radical must be critically self-aware in order to put the community worker alongside others. Walter Wink puts it well: "As we begin to acknowledge our own inner shadow, we become more tolerant of the shadow in others. As we begin to love the enemy within, we develop the compassion we need to love the enemy without."[8] Acknowledging our inner shadows and enemies locates us firmly in the camp of others. All of a sudden, the community worker-radical finds herself in solidarity with others.

4. A lack of appreciation

Community workers are people bent on changing the world. Fortunately, and unlike many Christians, they have the eyes to see where there is injustice and inequality. Unfortunately, that is often all they see. They go to their communities and neighborhoods and underline what is still sadly lacking in these places. This can have the effect of shaming a community to the point that they turn away from the community worker in embarrassment.

It is better to initially affirm all that is pleasing and worthy of appreciation in a community. It is important to make mention, for example, of all the good things that the community has already done, of the sacrificial efforts made by others, of the goodness of the people despite their circumstances. If we genuinely say a big YES to all the good that already exists in the community, the people will be more willing to hear the bad news, even the bad news about personal and social sin. That opens the way to talking about the difference that Jesus can make to both these evils.

In Jesus' encounter with the woman at the well (John 4), he knew that her immediate need was for water but that she also needed eternal life. John Perkins points out, however, that Jesus' first words were not, "You are a sinner. You need to accept me into your life. God loves you and has a wonderful plan for your life," or "If you have enough faith you can drink all the water you want." Instead, Jesus said to her, "Give me a drink of water." Perkins explains the significance of this:

He [Jesus] did not start by saying, "I can help you." He wanted her to know that she could help him. The Jews despised and separated themselves from the Samaritans, so by talking to her and asking for help–demonstrating she had something of value that she could share with him–Jesus affirmed her dignity and broke down the wall of distrust.[9]

5. A lack of awareness

In each community there is a story with many characters, one of whom is God. Because God is God, he got to the community or neighborhood before the community worker. God was there first; he has been and is fully present in the story of the community. Walter Brueggemann, an Old Testament scholar, says God is "the absent one who is so powerfully present."[10] Others call this the "hiddenness of God" in a community. The community worker must look for this God and try and discern where he has been and where he is currently at work, then follow him.

Many a worker is tempted to look for God in the extraordinary events of the community or with the big people of the place. But God is often found in the very ordinary things of life and with the "little" people. For example, in

the life of any given community there are many chance
events where things just happen to occur. The people of
the community put these down to coincidences. But a
sensitive community worker may be able to make the
connection between these so-called "chance events" and
God. In other words (I think these are the words of Walter Brueggemann), "coincidence takes the place of miracle as a signal of divine activity."

We can find a good scriptural backdrop for comparing
how God works "out there" by comparing Exodus with
the book of Esther. In the former God works through
extraordinary events, but in the latter God is not even
mentioned. Yet God is there in the ordinary events. This
kind of scriptural reading presupposes that we have the
eyes to see God. When we see God we can point him out
to others.

Furthermore, because God is there and is doing what
only God does best—converting people—evangelism is not
all up to us. For this reason Bishop John Taylor warns us
not to turn this divine initiative into a human enterprise.
In other words, evangelism, rightly understood, cannot
be reduced to some sales program where success is
dependent on our packaging of the product, nor can it be
likened to a military campaign where the marshalling of
resources and correct use of strategies is paramount.
These approaches say more about human effort than anything else.

Evangelism, rightly understood, is a mystery: the chief
source is grace and the chief actor the Holy Spirit. We
cannot control these or reduce them to technique. Furthermore, Taylor counsels, the attitude of "it all depends
on me" is an attitude "that is bedeviling both the practice
and theology of our mission in these days . . . [and it is]
precisely what Jesus forbade at the start of it all. They [the
disciples] must not go it alone. They must not think that

the mission is their responsibility."[11] We do well to heed these timely words.

Models

It is one thing for a Christian community worker to have the above set of attitudes, but these alone will not create a transformative movement in a community. The right model is also needed. The Methodists were called that because of John Wesley's insistence that they get the method right. And history tells us they did. Their methods or models made a movement that transformed not only the local communities of the United Kingdom but also the whole nation.[12]

Today, most community workers employ one of four models in their efforts to see people come to Christ through their community projects. I suggest that the first two are problematic, whereas the latter two have some merit.

1. The "means" model

This model makes social responsibility a means to evangelism. The thinking is that "hungry people cannot listen to our sermons," so we must feed them so they can listen. The plethora of community projects during our "awful mistake" period were created so people could hear our message.

This model breaks down at various points. First, Jesus told his disciples to do good and expect nothing in return (Luke 6:35)–including converts! Second, our experience is that when the poor sense they are being given something, the expectation that they must give something in return makes them feel used and abused. They equate us with a visit from corrupt politicians. Providing help to get a religious response smells of hypocrisy.

Alan Nichols, an Anglican priest who has worked in refugee camps, suggests that we offend "if we manipulate people's dependence on our support to get a religious response."[13] Nichols further states that "it is always unethical to manipulate other people or pressurise them to act against their will or their own interests. It is also contrary to the spirit of the gospel."[14]

But in many of our community projects, we do exactly that. We create cycles of dependency whereby the beneficiaries feel duty-bound to reciprocate by giving us what they perceive we desire most—their conversion. Under these conditions, you never know the real state of their spiritual lives. It is better that people come to Christ through faith and repentance, as suggested in the Scriptures, not through obligations created by community projects. Despite our best intentions, however, this model proved to be the one we followed in the early years.

2. The "love in action" model

This model points out that as we love, serve, help, give and live with the people, they will come to see why we are doing what we are doing. Through our "love in action" they will come to know God's love for them. You do not have to say anything—in fact, it is better that you don't. Our actions will speak louder than words.

But this model also breaks down. Our experience is that people invariably misinterpret our actions and get the wrong idea altogether. If we want a proper understanding of our actions we must make time for a verbal explanation. For the Christian, this eventually means drawing people away from what we have done and helping them to see what God has done through Jesus Christ. We moved unintentionally to this model.

3. The "provocative" model

This model advocates doing community projects in such a way that they provoke genuine questions from people. This idea has proven helpful. For example, when we moved away from projects that only benefitted a favored few and into those that benefitted the entire community, some people were amazed. They asked why we were helping people who obviously did not belong to our church or religion. When we asked the very poor and the least educated for their advice and help in implementing various projects, some people were puzzled and wondered why we should esteem the poor so highly.

And so it went on. Community concern and projects done in a prophetic and radical way will create a new set of questions in people. These questions give us an opportunity to give a reason for the hope that is within us. We see this clearly demonstrated in the life of Jesus. The things he did, and how he did them, so surprised people that they asked many questions of him about his background and motivation.

In order to provoke questions, community workers must do projects in a biblical, prophetic and radical way. This demands much study, brainstorming, creative energy and agonizing periods of trial and error. Quite unexpectedly, we hit on this model as we sought to do community development in a more appropriate way.

4. The "tandem" model

This model has not been our experience but is worthy of attention. Ron Sider, in his recent work on the relationship between evangelism and social action, tells of Bishop David Gitari and his work in Mt. Kenya East. Gitari places local evangelists trained to do evangelism and church planting in each parish he is responsible for. He also assigns community development workers in these parishes. Sider comments that the "result has been economic development and exploding church growth."[15]

Renewal

Putting the best models into practice will need an enormous commitment. Holism is a costly mandate with many demands.

First, it demands the courage to become someone we may never have been before and the courage to become a church that we may never have been before. It also demands the courage to continue to flow with our gifts and strengths, but also the courage to grow in our weaknesses. In other words, we must be willing to involve ourselves in those gifts and ministries that might threaten us or run contrary to our particular traditions. Holism is a risky and, at times, a reckless methodology.

Second, we must be contemplatives. We must be able to withdraw from the heat of the action and reflect on what is happening and how we should proceed. There is little place for leadership by lurching about or having knee-jerk reactions when engaging in unfamiliar paths of ministry. Instead, we must be contemplatives in action.

Third, to aid us in this contemplative activity we will need a canonical grasp of Scripture. We must have knowledge that is broad enough to glean biblical data and directives from all of Scripture and not just from our favorite or familiar books and passages. We must not fall into the temptation to use, for example, just the Exodus grid as some liberation theologians do, or just the prophetic grid as some radical Christians do, or just the kingdom grid as some of the charismatic third wavers do, or just the Pauline grid as some church growth proponents do, or just the Matthew 28 Commission as some missionary organizations do. Rather, we need all these and other grids if we are to take in what Scripture has to say to us about our holistic involvement.

Fourth, such a reading of Scripture and engagement with the world will demand that we be even more charismatic. We must have a broad communion with the Spirit where we not only hear him in areas relating to evangelism and church planting but also in ministries of justice-making and development.

Finally, we need to hear what the Spirit might be saying in areas with which we are unfamiliar. This may mean that we become more cooperative with other traditions and movements within the body of Christ, traditions that have heard things from the Spirit we have yet to hear. Working with the unfamiliar has a way of highlighting what is helpful within one's own tradition, but also what is lacking. Here we must open our tradition to what others can give us. A holistic walk is a communal affair. It demands that we humble ourselves and walk together.

Becoming more effective

It is my conviction that the mandate of holism is in danger of facing a crisis of effectiveness. Some Christians are struggling to believe that community projects can be an effective means of seeing people come to Christ. Most of us have either experienced, seen or heard of cases where very little evangelism resulted from community involvement. But if there has been one lesson I have learned over the years, it is to never let a bad example or experience rob me of the journey. Despite what I have seen or been through, the journey of involvement continues.

Be encouraged; those projects scoring high on success invariably undergo at least one major revision as a result of failure of part of the original plan. Paradoxically, error is essential to learning, mistake-making to problem-solving and even failure to success. If, therefore, our evangelism is proving ineffective alongside the community projects, then we should not abandon the latter, but use the crisis as a source of new information. It is time to reflect critically on our practice, no matter how painful or humbling this might be, so we can be more effective in our communities.

I hope that the five worker-related factors and the brief summary of the four models can be starting points for this process of critical reflection. If, after reflection, you discern a different and better way to go in your holistic ministry, then return to the streets and test it. If your new insight proves helpful, share it with the rest of us so that we too can enter the adventure.

Back to the story

We had come a long way since the awful mistake days of 1988 when, on the advice of the poor, we had dismantled just about everything we had done. It was now early 1993, and Ruby and I felt as though the bits and pieces of the jigsaw puzzle were finally fitting together. Our life was falling into place. But this time I was wary. Before 1988 I felt like this and look what happened. Surely, I hoped, we would not have to go through another crisis. But with God—and indeed the poor—there are many strange turnings, many surprises.

NOTES

1 Tokunboh Adeyemo, "A critical evaluation of contemporary perspectives" in Bruce J. Nicholls (ed.), *In Word and Deed: Evangelism and Social Responsibility* (Exeter: Paternoster Press, 1985), p. 54.

2 Ronald Sider, *Evangelism and Social Action* (1993), is a good introduction. If you are more inclined to an interactive approach to learning about this area, then an excellent video, book and tape workshop presentation is John Steward, *Biblical Holism: Where God, People and Deeds Connect* (East Burwood: World Vision Australia, 1994). I would also recommend Brian Hathaway, *Beyond Renewal: The Kingdom of God* (Milton Keynes: Word, 1990), and Murray Robertson, *The Future of Humanity* (Sutherland: Albatross, 1993). Two books that have helped me over the years have been Vinay Samuel and Christopher Sugden (eds.), *The Church in Response to Human Need* (Grand Rapids: Eerdmans, 1987) and Bruce J. Nicholls (ed.), *In Word and Deed* (1985).

3 Raymond Fung, *Evangelistically Yours: Ecumenical Letters on Contemporary Evangelism* (Geneva: WCC Publications, 1992), p. 12.

4 Ibid., p. 12.

5 Bosch, *Transforming Mission*, p. 138.

6 Fung, p. 12.

7 Ibid., p. 12f.

8 Walter Wink, *Engaging the Powers: Discernment and Resistance in a World of Domination* (Minneapolis: Fortress Press, 1992), p. 267.

9 John M. Perkins, *Beyond Charity: The Call to Christian Community Development* (Grand Rapids: Baker Book House, 1993), p. 33.

10 Walter Brueggemann, *Power, Providence and Personality: Biblical Insight into Life and Ministry* (Kentucky: John Knox Press, 1990), p. 80.

11 John V. Taylor, *The Go-between God: The Holy Spirit and the Christian Mission* (London: SCM Press, 1972), p. 3.

12 Howard A. Snyder, *Signs of the Spirit: How God Reshapes the Church* (Grand Rapids: Zondervan, 1989) further describes the methods employed by Wesley.

13 Alan Nichols et. al., *Risks in Christian Witness: Ethical Issues in International Development and Urban Mission* (East Burwood: World Vision Australia), p. 10.

14 Ibid., p. 21.

15 Sider, *Evangelism and Social Action*, p. 21.

Discipleship and a Debt of Gratitude

The Levite, the Priest and the Good Samaritan all saw the wounded man on the side of the road. But the latter did what the other two would not—he went to the man. Going to our neighbor on the roadside of life is not separate from our spiritual walk.

In 1985 we went to our poor neighbors in the slums of Manila. To do that we had to actually get on a plane, go to Manila and walk into a slum. This was far from an easy walk. It was marked by much loss—the loss of comfortable New Zealand, our friends and family. In 1986, it was the loss of health as we came down with one virus and illness after another. That same year the loss of security frightened us as we came face to face with danger like never before. In 1987 we lost our son, Joseph. He lived for three weeks before his life was cut short by a virus that invaded Ruby during her pregnancy. The next year saw the loss of much ministry. The poor of our slum told us to close everything down: the clinics, church, loan bank, mercy ministries, infrastructure projects, income generation projects. We had done development in an inappropriate way that was causing much social breakdown in the community. It had to stop. Overnight, 75 percent of the "Christians" left the church.

These losses rendered me bankrupt. I started to lose my faith and became profoundly disillusioned, filled with deep disappointment and personal anguish. I lost confidence in my past. The years of training, reading, prayer and obedience made no difference in the face of absolute poverty. I began to distrust the voices that had guided my past and in doing so lost my shame. During this long dark night of the soul, I came close to doing some stupid things.

At the end of 1988 we left Manila for our sabbatical in Oxford, England. While there I recaptured some of my evangelical roots and gained an understanding of why we had lost so many things over the years. We returned to Manila in 1990, and during the next two years experienced the joy of success.

In 1992 the lament of loss could again be heard on our lips. A woman that we had worked with for years, who had been set free from evil forces and had become a Christian, confessed to us that she had returned to prostitution. She was selling her body so she could build a house. The next year brought more of the same.

The final nail in the coffin came with the terrible and tragic disclosure about Tony, the Filipino pastor that I had seen converted, and had discipled over the past several years. He had stolen money from his poor neighbors and fled the slum. I have not seen him since. His fall had terrible consequences, the worst of which was the breakup of the small group he was leading, which we had seen develop into a "face to face" community. The shame of Tony's disgrace was too much for it to carry. The group's reputation had been blighted forever. Sin in such closely knit poor communities cannot be hidden away. Sin is social in these places and has public consequences.

That same year, a court order was handed down to our slum warning them of an impending eviction and demolition. All of our work would be lost to the bulldozers and reduced to rubble. We would lose our past and the poor would lose their future. The poor always come off second-best after a demolition.

A most unexpected loss

Finally, in 1994, we sensed it was time to leave the organization that we had been working with and leading over the years. This was a most painful experience as we had gone through much blood, sweat and tears with these people. We had been one of the founding couples of this mission. In fact, we were the first Servants family to attempt to live in a slum.

Many factors influenced our decision. Most of the things we had started were quite unexpectedly being brought to natural points of closure. Many of the ministries we had helped to start were in the hands of others. The community development projects were already in the hands of the poor. I had also handed over the leadership of the Servants Manila Team to others. Our work in Damayan Lagi was coming to an end. Ruby had handed over the management of the embroidery exporting business to others. There was little that we were still actively involved with and we wondered what next we could do with Servants.

We were also having some philosophical difficulties with the Servants organization. Ruby and I felt that Servants was going in a different direction from the one we felt led to follow. We felt Servants was following a course we considered was not an appropriate expression of mission and development in the Two-Thirds World. After much heart-searching we felt it was better that Servants go their way and we go ours. We left on the best of terms. Our differences were not personal but professional.

It was to take more than a year for me to get over this decision. I grieved for the big part of me that Servants had become. Many tears were shed. It was all most unexpected and for that reason very disappointing. From the outset, I had wanted to walk with Servants for twenty years or more. Instead, our journey was cut short after only nine.

I learned many invaluable lessons from this experience. First and foremost, we are to be disciples of our Lord Jesus and not disciples of a person, institution or model. Looking back, I think I had become too emotionally attached to Servants, its members and its mandate. When we align ourselves excessively to something, it becomes increasingly difficult to hear other things that God might be saying to us. I believe Ruby and I had a part in the building of Servants and are so thankful for that privilege. But it seemed God wanted to continue to build Servants without us. We are confident that he will.

But leaving Servants raised a new set of questions. Should we stay in the Philippines? Was it time to leave Damayan Lagi? Could we leave after all that had happened?

Three factors led us to believe it was right to leave Manila. First, our work in Damayan Lagi was coming to an end. We had finished much of what we had started. Second, Ruby and I were beginning to feel uncomfortable about the number of missionaries in the Philippines. It is a country with a very strong national church, whether Catholic or Protestant, and which has, for some time, assumed the responsibility of reaching its people and country. Over the years we had counselled many not to come to the Philippines for this reason. We felt we had to back our words with our own departure.

We also wondered if it was time to return our children to the West so they could get to know New Zealand. To their credit, Emily (11), Thomas (9) and Joanna (5) all said they were flexible and would stay if that was what we wanted.

Finally, we left because we believed God was calling us back to New Zealand. For some time we had wondered whether the storm front of mission had moved from the Two-Thirds World, where so much growth was taking place, and had shifted to the nations of the so-called First World that were being afflicted by secularization, modernity and a widening gap between rich and poor. Unlike the Two-Thirds World, there was no strong church in place to engage these problems. The church in New Zealand and other developed countries seemed to be dying. Ruby and I could see that there was a struggle in New Zealand and we could have a part to play in that struggle.

We had been talking with our friends in Damayan Lagi for some time about these issues, so they were prepared for our decision to leave. After many official and unofficial functions, the day of final goodbyes came. It was confusing. It would take us six months to deal with the emotions of that day. Our poor neighbors took us to the airport and with much crying we walked into the terminal and headed for New Zealand.

Michael and Ruby Duncan

The years had taken their toll. We had experienced the loss of New Zealand, friends, family, health and security, a baby, ministry, shame, colleagues in the ministry; and we had given years of hard work.

The company we keep

Since returning to New Zealand the losses have continued. In many respects, our walk of discipleship continues to be one of loss. Far from the neat and tidy Christianity that is often preached from the comfort of a pulpit, our discipleship has been one of confusion, contradiction, chaos and conflict. It is a discipleship of loose ends. The reaction of others to our story has often been, "This can't be right!" Some have even had the audacity to suggest that maybe we did not pray enough. For the record, we prayed at least two to three hours a day for most of those years. Living and working in difficult places of discipleship demands a rigorous prayer life.

Other folk have wondered whether our story of loss said more about me than anything else, as though I was somewhat "off the wall" or cursed in some way. If so, I find myself in good company. A fellow traveller on this road of costly discipleship once wrote,

> *I have worked much harder, been in prison more frequently, been flogged more severely, and been exposed to death again and again. Five times I received from the Jews the forty lashes minus one. Three times I was beaten with rods, once I was stoned, three times I was shipwrecked, I spent a night and a day in the open sea, I have been constantly on the move. I have been in danger from rivers, in danger from bandits, in danger from my own countrymen, in danger from Gentiles; in danger in the city, in danger in the country, in danger at sea; and in danger from false brothers. I have labored and toiled and have often gone without sleep; I have known hunger and thirst and have*

*often gone without food; I have been cold and naked (2
Corinthians 11:23-27).*

A careful rereading of Paul's life reveals that very little
is said of his first sixteen years in the ministry. We are
given no record of any success that he may have enjoyed
during those years. Possibly these were wilderness years
for Paul. He spent considerable time with the church at
Corinth but this church proved to be very difficult. Over
the years he endured the pain of division and separation,
especially with Peter, James and Barnabas.

The discipleship of loss is disturbingly scriptural. I
have had more pain and suffering as a Christian than I
ever did as a non-Christian. For me those pre-Christian
years were marked by a broken family, drug dealing and
usage and Eastern mysticism. But the pain in God's service need not surprise us. If the gospel cost Jesus his life,
then surely that same gospel will also cost us dearly. But
the question I am repeatedly asked is, "How do you keep
going in the light of such loss?"

We are still following our Lord Jesus. Upon arriving in
New Zealand we relocated to one of the poorer suburbs
of Wellington, the capital city. Our income is below the
poverty line for New Zealand and our house is very basic.
At the time of writing this book I am working with a
Christian organization that is involved with marginalized
ethnic minority groups and communities.

The debt of gratitude

So how do we keep going? It is not out of sheer determination—this quickly fails when one is serving in difficult
places. It is not, as has been suggested to me, because I
am trying to work out some deep neurosis that I picked
up in my troubled pre-Christian days. We do not continue because we have been commanded to. God is a

God who commands, but we are often too ready to apply "command language" to the things we do. We end up with a bellowing God who drives us. Christians who have that kind of God invariably end up resenting him.

For us, the secret of continuing is found in Paul's life. In the last letter he ever wrote he twice declared to Timothy that he had been "shown mercy." More often than not, you do not see Paul being commanded into mission. Instead, we read of Paul engaging in mission out of a deep sense of gratitude to the Father. Paul was overwhelmed by all that God had done in Christ for him and his only response was that of gratitude expressed in mission. Paul could do nothing but mission in light of the fact that Jesus had given himself for Paul (Galatians 2:20), and that God's love had been poured into Paul's heart (Galatians 5:5). David Bosch writes:

> He [Paul] has exchanged the terrible debt of sin for another debt, the debt of gratitude, which manifests itself in mission.[1]

For Paul, the joy of his salvation was still very much alive years after his conversion to Christ. It is when we lose the joy of our salvation that we also lose the sense of gratitude to the Father that has been shown as a key motivational category for mission. So it was that my wife became a Christian in 1972 and I followed in 1976. We both received forgiveness, reconciliation, redemption, grace, love and healing. Our Father has been so excessively generous with us. And it is this grace of God that compels us to serve him no matter the loss or cost.

The act of worship

Following this generous God is not easy. After our sabbatical in 1989 we were set to return to Manila. One night I was awakened by my wife's crying. She did not want to return to the slums of Manila—they could hardly be considered the will of God for anyone, poor or missionary. Her honesty caused me to confess my own very real reluctance to return.

Yet again we found ourselves in good company. We read of Ezekiel, who after an exhilarating time of worship was taken up and sent to the exiles. It was the manner of his going that encouraged us. Ezekiel went "in bitterness and in the anger of [his] spirit, with the strong hand of the Lord upon [him]" (Ezekiel 3:14). Similarly, Jesus asked the Father to take the cup from him as he contemplated going to his difficult place of discipleship—the place of the Skull (Luke 22:42).

Going to these difficult places of discipleship is not something that we naturally and necessarily want to do. We must not fall into the trap of reducing the call of God and his will to something that we want to do. That is a subversion of the call of Christ. Rather, it should be out of a deep sense of gratitude to the Father for all that he has given us in Christ that we will want to go to the dark corners of our planet.

More and more I am becoming convinced that berating and lashing ourselves and others to get involved in mission is not the way to go. It is as we return to the merciful Father that we will then turn to our neighbor. It is knowing God that leads to knowing others. In other words, worship leads to mission. As we worship the God of mercy so we become merciful toward others. In a very real sense, you become what you worship. In worshipping God we end up loving what he loves. And God loves the world (John 3:16) and loves justice (Isaiah 61:8).

We keep going not because of who we are but because of who God is. In the final analysis, enduring in costly mission says more about knowing God's character than it does about relying on our character. In hearing our particular story so many people have commented that we must be saints and amazing people to have gone to the slums in the first place, and then to have endured all that we have and emerge still in love with Jesus and wanting to follow him.

Ruby and I are very ordinary people. I think many of the struggles I have alluded to bear witness to that. We do what we do not because of who we are, but because of who God is and what he has done in Christ for us. It is this reality that has compelled many people throughout the ages to walk into places of difficult discipleship no matter the cost.

I am reminded of the replacement couples for the missionaries who died in Africa (see chapter 8). Their commitment to the cross was echoed by another missionary of the day, who argued "that if Christ be God and died for me, then no sacrifice can be too great for me to make for him."

NOTES

1 Bosch, *Transforming Mission*, p. 138.

MARC

Bringing you key resources on the world mission of the church

MARC books and other publications support the work of MARC (Mission Advanced Research and Communications Center), which is to inspire fresh vision and empower Christian mission among those who extend the whole gospel to the whole world.

Recent MARC titles include:

▶ *Signs of Hope in the City*, Robert C. Linthicum. Christian leaders from around the world discuss the critical issues that will surround urban mission in the 21st century. $7.95

▶ *Serving with the Poor in Asia: Cases in Holistic Ministry*, T. Yamamori, B. Myers and D. Conner, editors. Well-known mission leaders comment on cases in holistic mission presented from seven different Asian contexts. These cases and analyses help us better understand what a holistic witness to the gospel of Christ means today. $15.95

▶ *God So Loves the City: Seeking a Theology for Urban Mission*, Charles Van Engen and Jude Tiersma, editors. Experienced urban practitioners from around the world explore the most urgent issues facing those who minister in today's cities in search of a theology for urban mission. $21.95

▶ *By Word, Work and Wonder*, Thomas H. McAlpine. Examines the question of holism in Christian mission and brings you several case studies from around the world that will push your thinking on this important topic. $15.95

▶ *The Changing Shape of World Mission* by Bryant L. Myers. Presents in color graphs, charts and maps the challenge before global missions, including the unfinished task of world evangelization. Also available in color slides and overheads—excellent for presentations!

Book. . . . .$ 5.95
Slides. . . . .$ 99.95
Overheads. . . . .$ 99.95
Presentation Set *(one book, slides and overheads)* $175.00

Order Toll Free in USA: 1-800-777-7752
Visa and MasterCard accepted

MARC A division of World Vision International
121 E. Huntington Dr. • Monrovia • CA • 91016-3400

Ask for the MARC Newsletter and complete publications list

LINCOLN CHRISTIAN COLLEGE AND SEMINARY

TWO INTERACTIVE VIDEO WORKSHOPS

from John Steward

BIBLICAL HOLISM

Where God, People and Deeds Connect

The fruit of John Steward's personal journey to understand how God works through his people. This workshop focuses on the biblical roots of holism and how holism impacts our life and ministry. The video includes interview segments with Tony Campolo, Frances O'Gorman and Brian Hathaway.

THE GIFT THAT RELEASES

First Steps in People-Centred Development

The culmination of many lessons World Vision has learned through the years of struggling with the poor and marginalized. In this video, John Steward facilitates a multi-cultural group that engages in role playing designed to provide affirmation and new ideas about development. The focus is on empowerment and change, while giving many case studies.

WORKSHOP CONTENTS

◆ 3-hour interactive video
◆ Comprehensive workbook, study guide, resource manual & facilitator's guide
◆ Two 90-minute audio tapes
◆ Wallchart (for *The Gift That Releases* only)

PRICES

◆ Video Workshops:

Biblical Holism E-015 $149.95

The Gift That Releases ... E-020 $149.95

◆ Books .... $ 24.95

(prices are identical for both workshops. Quantity discounts are available for books—call for info.)

Order Toll Free: 1-800-777-7752 Fax: (818)301-7786 E-Mail: MARCpubs@wvi.org